ANYONE CAN RUN

ANYONE CAN RUN

JOAN GERAGHTY

CURRACH
PRESS

THIS BOOK RECORDS ANECDOTAL ACCOUNTS OF RUNNING EXPERIENCES, ALONG
WITH SOME SPORTING TIPS AND INSIGHTS.
IT IS NOT INTENDED FOR USE AS A PROFESSIONAL TRAINING GUIDE.
READERS ARE WELCOME TO CONTACT THE AUTHOR
BY EMAIL: JOANGERAGHTY@GMAIL.COM.

First published in 2008 by
CURRACH PRESS
55A Spruce Avenue, Stillorgan Industrial Park, Blackrock, Co. Dublin
www.currach.ie

1 3 5 4 2

Cover by Blurtt
Origination by Currach Press
Printed by Betaprint, Bluebell Industrial Estate, Dublin 12
ISBN: 978 1 85607 955 6
The author has asserted her moral rights.

FOR NATHAN, PETER, HELEN AND MARY

Acknowledgements

For making this book possible, my thanks to Jo O'Donoghue and Currach Press, who understood the worth of the theme in hand and encouraged me along the way. Back to basics, I want to thank my Dad and Mum, Richard and Beda Tobin, for continuing to be fantastic role models for longevity and vitality and for nurturing my love for words and writing and supporting me and my education through many, many years. Thanks also to all my siblings (especially the older ones), who tested my competitive spirit over the decades and kept me constantly on my toes.

I wish to pay special tribute to my dear friend and colleague, Helen Kelleher, who from the off in our joint journalism careers has always believed in me. You are much appreciated, Helen. My thanks also to my many colleagues in the media world for continuing to support my writing career and to all my friends who have been there for me at various stages in my life.

Of course this book would never have happened without the *Mayo News*, the local newspaper in which I have been honing my writing skills since 1995. My thanks to former editor, Sean Staunton, who taught me many hard lessons in the ways of the media/political/business world. Thank you, Sean, for all the time you invested in me.

My thanks also to current *Mayo News* editor, Denise Horan, for giving me the space to develop my writing, and to proprietor, Dermot Berry, for facilitating my career. Special tribute also to the late Joe Berry, a fantastic supporter over the years.

To my husband, Padraic, who has been by my side and always there for me. I don't deserve you. Thanks,P! Also to Granny Kathleen, who has been a rock to us in our family life and all my in-laws and family. It's a blessing having such support. To our wonderful children, Nathan, Peter, Helen and Mary – it's because of you we can still joyfully experience each new day.

In regard to the workings of this book, I am grateful to Michael and Joanne Lennon of the wonderful family/eco-friendly Westport Woods Hotel and Adventure Centre. Both my running and the book came together in this fine establishment, starting in the hotel's Beech Club gym and leisure centre. Thanks also to the many friendly staff members at the Beech Club, especially Paul. To my running buddy, sparring partner and friend, Noreen O'Toole, let's keep on chugging (not so fast, Noreen!).

Last but not least, I wish to record my appreciation of the people of my native Castlebar and adopted town of Westport, who keep the mind humming with their endless energy and constant drive to live life to the full. It's a privilege and an inspiration to live in such a beautiful and burgeoning part of the world.

Joan Geraghty, December 2007

CONTENTS

Foreword

Ray D'Arcy

Starting running is a big thing. For a lot of people running for five minutes would kill them but it's easier than many things. Swimming and other sports involve a lot of extra hassle. You have to get into the car and get to the gym or pool first of all or maybe meet up with teammates on a pitch. But with running, all you need is yourself to start training.

Contrary to what you'd believe on those evenings when you're slouching on the couch, feeling lethargic, that is exactly the time you need to get out and have a run. It will actually energise you – which is the opposite to what common sense would tell you.

As with most things, once you start doing it yourself you begin to notice it around you. From talking to people I think more of us are running. We're more health-conscious now – or maybe people look at me and think that I'm a bit of a naffer, because that's what I used to think about other people out running.

After a while of running regularly, you miss it if you don't do it. You can get quite irritable if you go a few days without, which might not seem particularly good, but you could be addicted to worse things.

For a long time with running, I found the first three miles hell. But then there was a period in the middle of training for the marathon where I was doing the long runs and it was lovely. I would be coasting and had a rhythm going. But then at the end, with all the extra mileage, it becomes difficult again.

I think, with exercise, you reach a level of fitness where if you lose it, your body tells you. It sends you warning signs that you need to get back to that same level again. It's not always possible. It is effort and you do have to get out there on days you'd prefer not to. But when you make that effort, you feel way better for it.

I try to run twice a week now with a long run in that. I cycle in and out nine miles each way for work during the week so I'm getting some sort of exercise every day. It's hugely important for me to be active. I think it keeps me sane. I'm cycling into work five years now and it's got to the stage where I hate when I can't do it if, say, I have to get into a suit and take the car. That bugs me all day.

But I wouldn't see myself as some sort of exercise junkie. With the daily cycling, there's more to it than the exercise. You arrive into work and you're refreshed. The wind has blown up your hair – whatever hair you have – it's taken you 35–40 minutes and you feel alive.

A lot of my friends think I'm mad that I exercise as much as I do but then I look at people who do things like the 'Iron Man' event and think that they're the nutters. I do like to do challenging runs; for instance I have been doing ten miles a week regularly. I can see myself doing half-marathons regularly too because they're doable. I did the Phoenix Park last year in 1 hour 37 minutes.

I suppose I'm an exercise evangelist. I think we're selling the fight against obesity wrongly to people. It shouldn't be about the size of your dress or your waist, but about how you feel. For a person five or six stone overweight, the goal of the size-12 dress or the 34-inch waist is so far away. But if you can get them to exercise in some small way so they produce the endorphins that make them feel good, that should be the priority. Then they get hooked on that feeling. So I don't think we sell the positive, medical advantages of exercise to people. It's all about weight when it shouldn't be about that.

While running isn't my first love, the highs from it can't be bettered. The big thing for me with running is that I didn't like it, but now I do. Now if I've a spare 45 minutes I can get five miles or whatever in and that's brilliant. What else do you get done in 45 minutes?

After the marathon, I knew I'd be running for the rest of my life because once I achieved that and then went out running again, I felt, yeah, this suits me fine. I'm not doing it for any particular reason but it makes me feel good and gives me some head space.

Introduction

Two years ago I started running and I haven't stopped since. Obviously, I don't mean that literally as there have been plenty of stops and starts in between with some breaks going on for weeks at a time. But in broad terms, I have kept at it, shuffling one foot after the other along highways and byways or on treadmills at gyms, with the result that I am now addicted to the activity.

Developing a passion for running was something I couldn't have anticipated as it had never interested me before. The fact that I was no spring chicken when I took to it made it even more unlikely, as I felt surely I must be too old to be seen out and about extending my limbs in such a manner.

Being a mother of four small children also confused the issue as I wondered whether it was wrong of me to invest so much time in improving my body and fitness at a stage when our offspring needed me around the clock. Thankfully, such concerns quickly fizzled out as it became clear that running and parenthood make a terrific partnership. Not only was running proving beneficial to me but to everyone who came into contact with me because of the happy state of mind it left me in.

Any preconception I had that running might be a man's sport was easily dispensed with too. While men certainly outnumber women as passionate followers of the sport, the gap is closing, as female runners – young and old, mothers, aunts and grannies – swell the ranks of runners right around the world.

There are regular running fixtures all over Ireland, and the number of 5k, 10k, half- and full marathon events is increasing all the time. Athletic clubs are also recognising the trend and accommodating fun-runners.

Over the course of my running journey to date, I have learned a great deal about it as an exercise, and so much about myself in the process, that I love everything associated with it. Becoming a runner has definitely made me a better person in many ways, by giving me discipline and direction and providing me with an excellent resource for venting frustration, anxiety and other negative emotions that can make life difficult. Just going for a run gives you space in your head to work things through and to appreciate all the good things in life. The longer you run, the more problems get sorted, so that by the time you arrive home, everything is grand again.

I was forty years of age when I took up running and at the time I didn't really think it was going to work for me. My interest in the activity was based solely on my desire to become more active and the fact that it kept coming up as *the* exercise for anyone wanting to get fit. But I had clear memories of having tried a spot of running years before, and hating it. What I found particularly difficult was the sheer effort required to keep going.

The funny thing is that it was precisely this need to persevere that attracted me to running the second time around. I had been feeling overweight after having babies and got to a stage where I really wanted to push myself again. Having managed to overcome the desire to stop in my tracks on my first few outings, I soon started longing to exert myself further. After a while of regularly managing to run for five minutes non-stop, the next challenge was to stretch it out a little bit more.

As a high-intensity exercise, running is relentless. You have to keep going, without stopping, to reach your goal. There are no breaks. It isn't running if you stop. But keeping going brings huge rewards. Wonderful, natural highs follow most runs. If you've exerted yourself for a sustained period and really pushed hard physically, a wave of feel-good endorphins washes over you, leaving you feeling contented and terrific for at least the rest of the day. Your body temperature remains high for hours afterwards. You literally feel yourself buzzing with life and energy and enjoy knowing that your metabolism has been boosted. You consequently take greater pleasure from eating good food, acknowledging it for what it really is – essential fuel to keep your body performing well. You also seem to enjoy improved concentration and clarity of mind after challenging exercise, which always strikes me as a thank-you from the mind for giving the body the workouts it loves.

Even on non-training days, the benefits of running carry through, as muscles need rest to recover, grow and build up energy stores for the next outing. As rest is so crucial, it is one of the biggest rewards in training that you can really enjoy your days off.

It took a good six months for me to be fully bitten by the running bug, which, when it takes hold, can be powerfully addictive. As I enjoyed increasing natural highs following the sheer exertion of every run, I also started developing sufficient confidence to set new goals. I could happily have stayed at the level I was for a while, running two to three miles on the treadmill or outdoors a few times a week, but I felt it was in me to go that bit further. I also became aware of how important it is to keep making new goals in order to stay motivated.

After completing my first 5k fun-run, the notion of some day running a half-marathon suddenly seemed feasible. Of course I was aware that the ultimate goal for distance runners is to run a full marathon but whether my own experiences would stretch that far very much remained to be seen.

The reality is, running is hard. It can be difficult to keep going at it because your mental and physical form is different every day. You can feel fantastic on your Monday run and end it looking forward to your next outing on Wednesday but by the time that day comes around you may not want to run at all. Having to get out there and move all over again can feel like hell. This same pattern can go on for weeks and months on end. Whole periods of the year can go by where you think you must really hate running, because it feels so hard to do it all the time. You question whether you should even bother sticking with it but know you can't give it up. If you do, it will create too great a hole in your life for you to deal with and deprive you of one of your most powerful anti-ageing and life-enhancing tools – a fit body.

Because running is so addictive and the real drug comes from the feel-good highs afterwards, you come to understand that it is the endorphins that keep you hooked. The only way to stay enjoying those wonderful after-run wellbeing feelings is to keep running. Diversifying into other sports might suit some people but for many, running is the only worthwhile activity. A suggestion at this point might be to change things round a bit. Join a running club, go work out with a running buddy, include more cross-training with weights and equipment at the gym, or sign up for a triathlon which will get you training in swimming and cycling as well.

Speed-training sessions can be hugely rewarding too because running shorter distances but in faster times brings a new sense of elation and moves your training from aerobic to anaerobic mode (without oxygen), where you are going too fast to use oxygen as fuel and must call on your own body reserves instead. It's hard to keep improving your personal best (PB) all the time with constant endurance running but with speed-training, you can up your average speed and stay at an improved level for the long term.

The fact is you will hit a plateau every now and then: changing your training pattern will prevent you getting stale and help maintain a sense of novelty.

As things turned out, my running course was far from smooth. Several unanticipated hiccups along the way slowed my progress considerably, including soft-tissue injuries and aching joints which forced me to take breaks. At one point my health became such an issue that I thought I might even have to give up running entirely. I was amazed to discover that having to entertain that possibility affected me deeply. It actually felt like grieving a loss. That is how hard the running bug can affect you once it bites.

Over the course of training, as I became fitter and stronger, my whole outlook on life and the world at large changed dramatically. Everything improved: my presence of mind, my energy levels, my body and my perception of it; my relationships with family, our children and friends; my attitude towards work and my work performance itself. Most of all, my interests changed, in that I became more health-conscious and developed a deep interest in fitness.

While my running was purely of the 'fun' variety, in that my aim was personal satisfaction and not medals for speed, I identified new role models in athletes and those who regularly worked out. I admired toned physiques for the evidence they showed of so much effort and exertion, and aspired to making my own body as lean and athletic as possible.

What really excited me was watching other runners out and about. People I had never noticed before suddenly caught my eye, and I loved coming across the odd veteran runner along the highways and byways, especially those who seemed to sprint the whole way. To me, running was always a struggle, whereas to them, it appeared effortless. I marvelled at this and wondered if I would ever be able to make it look easy too.

My age didn't come into it at all and I was heartened by a little nugget of information I picked up from a running manual along the way, which stated that a person taking up serious running for the first time can expect to keep improving their performance for at least seven years, no matter what age they start.

Fortunately, my husband Padraic also took up running shortly after me and developed a similar passion for the activity. He managed to run his first half-marathon before me, having taken my place at an event I had to forego due to health problems. We both became very interested in all things running and fitness, and started following related sports coverage. At our age, obviously we weren't interested in becoming professional athletes. We wanted to get fit and stay that way.

Even though running confers so many excellent health and anti-ageing benefits on a person, there is no denying that a lot of time and effort must be invested before these rewards can be reaped. The real secret to becoming a runner is to actually get out there and do it regularly. Even long-term runners will tell you that lengthy breaks can jeopardise an entire running career. Just a few weeks off exercise can knock your fitness levels back to zero and having to start from scratch again can take a whole lot more motivation and commitment.

But with constant training, you can't help getting better. As a result, your self-confidence grows with every new goal reached and your sense of achievement blossoms. The compliments you inevitably receive from people along the way help enormously too. As your fitness improves, your muscles become stronger and more toned, body fat burns away and you look much better and younger. It's all part and parcel of committing to a regular exercise regime and once you get a taste of feeling good about yourself again, you'll want to keep working on that feeling.

In my own case, I had been looking for an outlet to help me feel better about my pretty stressful life but would never have guessed such a high-intensity exercise would fill this need. I now know I still like challenging myself physically and can push myself harder all the time. As someone with a busy family and work life, having to depend only on myself every time I feel like a run makes it a dream escape valve. It is the perfect antidote to the stresses of modern-day living.

There are some people who argue that what I call 'running' should really be termed 'jogging' in most instances but I have read that the distinction between jogging and running is that the former involves moving the legs at a rate a little faster than speed walking (6km-7km an hour), whereas running starts from 8km an hour and upwards.

I'd like to think that my average pace now is 10km an hour, which qualifies me as the runner I claim to be.

Considering that Paula Radcliffe ran an average of 12 miles (16km) an hour over the entire course of her 2-hour 15-minute world record London marathon in 2003, this clearly does not make me an athlete. It is precisely for this reason that I decided to write this book, believing as a non-athlete how important it is to highlight how good running for fun, pleasure and personal achievement can be.

I consider myself privileged to have turned the corner and survived that gruelling phase where everything about running was unpleasant. Now I look forward to every new run, long or short, in happy anticipation. I'm not bothered whether it is wet or dry, hot or cold outside. I temper my run to suit the conditions of the time and if it's too wild or stormy, there's always the gym to work out in.

No matter how busy you may be, making time for running is

a very worthwhile exercise. If you are lucky enough to have your health and an able body, you too might like to give it a try. Even if you feel you've let things slide on the physical side, remember the body has wonderful restorative powers. It can regenerate strength, vigour and vitality as soon as you start setting it in motion again. It is simply a fallacy to believe that old age and physical deterioration must go hand in hand. Keep moving and you'll stay young.

I hope you enjoy reading my own personal running log to date as well as the fascinating stories of the other runners featured here. Be inspired.

Profiles of Featured Runners

Ernie Caffrey

Ernie Caffrey, 71, is a former politician who served his town and county (Ballina and County Mayo), as a public representative from 1985. He was a Senator in Dáil Eireann from 1997 to 2002 and over the course of a number of years, led a sedentary life attending meetings and travelling long journeys by car. In 2006, at the age of 69, Ernie took up walking in an effort to lose weight and get fit. One year later he was a champion sprinter after winning the 60-metre dash in the masters' category at the All Ireland Masters' Championships in Nenagh. During a typical training session, Ernie likes to run up to at least 15mph at three-minute intervals on his treadmill, which is built on a steel base that 'bounces to give the feeling of being out on the road'. A white line painted across this novel structure, designed by the man himself, shows exactly how many metres Ernie covers in each workout. A little clock, strategically placed above, assists Ernie in monitoring his ever-improving form.

Grainne Cunningham

Grainne Cunningham, 40, is a journalist with the *Irish Independent*, based in Killiney, who has run two Dublin City marathons to date (with finishing swim times of 4 hours 21 minutes and 4 hours 17 minutes). She and her husband Simon Bradshaw have triplet boys, Jack, Harry and Luca, born in December 2004. Running has become even more important to Grainne since becoming a mother of three. She is currently experimenting with mountain-running and speed training and while she has no immediate plans to run a third marathon, she isn't ruling another one out.

Ray D'Arcy

Ray D'arcy, 43, is a presenter of the popular *Ray D'Arcy Show* on Today FM. A native of Kildare, he and his partner Jenny celebrated the birth of their daughter, Kate, in 2006. The keep-fit fan who took up running in 2003 after announcing on air that he would do a triathlon in 2004, went to the trouble of importing a baby-jogger to sustain his running training after baby Kate was born. In 2005, Ray ran his first Dublin City Marathon in 3 hours 41 minutes. He cycles in and out to work – 18 miles every day – and, having learned to swim the year before his fortieth birthday in 2004, remains a swimming enthusiast today.

Gerry Galvin

Gerry Galvin, 41, is a passionate runner who can be spotted most days on the highways and byways of his adopted town of Westport, County Mayo running up to or beyond a half-marathon at a time. The County Laois native and former hurler cuts a dashing figure with his long, graceful, stride, running at a pace which is always so fast and smooth that it looks effortless. Gerry, who works as a wall-chaser, is married to Mary and the couple have four young children. He has run three marathons to date, his fastest in 3 hours 5 minutes at the 2007 Dublin City Marathon, and is now working towards achieving a sub-three-hour time.

Mary Kennedy

Mary Kennedy is a household name in Ireland, having carved out a successful presenting career with RTÉ television, including the current *Nationwide* programme. Running has played an important role in Mary's life since she was a teenager, and she ran the third-ever Dublin City Marathon in 1981 in a time of 3 hours 40 minutes. Almost 20 years later, in 2000, she completed it again in a very respectable time of 4 hours 20 minutes. She tries to fit in three or four runs a week, of at least 30 minutes each.

Dr Mick Loftus
Dr Mick Loftus, 78, has been a GP in his home town of Crossmolina, County Mayo, for over 40 years and is deeply involved in numerous community and national organisations. He is is also known nationally for his campaigning against the association of alcohol with sport. He represented his home county at junior and senior GAA levels in the 1940s and 1950s, serving as President of the GAA during the 1980s. Weighing in at 15 stone on his sixtieth birthday, he vowed to become physically fit once more and took up walking before progressing to running. This active septuagenarian now runs three miles five times a week. In 2006, Dr Loftus won gold in the 3,000 metre race at the World Senior Games in Utah, as well as three silver medals in the 800, 1,500 and 5,000 metre races.

Professor Risteárd Mulcahy
Retired cardiologist Risteárd Mulcahy took up running in his fifties, running his first marathon at the age of 60 and his third marathon aged 74. At the age of 63, he took 30 minutes off his best marathon time, finishing in 3 hours and 50 minutes.

Now 85, Professor Mulcahy, who headed up the cardiology department and heart disease research unit at St Vincent's University Hospital in Dublin for many years, still practises as a physician in the Charlemont Clinic, Ranelagh. He is a long-time advocate of exercise, recommending regular aerobic workouts for good health and mind. He has written an excellent book on the topic, *Improving with Age* (Liberties Press, 2004) and continues to practise what he preaches, dedicating much of his leisure time to power-walking and regular 18-hole rounds of golf.

Mary Walsh

Mary Walsh, 43, is a physiotherapist based in her native town of Westport, County Mayo. An avid runner, for many years she has combined her love of voluntary work, travel and running as part of a varied, exciting and fulfilling lifestyle. She has run three charity marathons with Croí, all in New York, finishing all three around the 3 hour 44 minute mark.

1

GETTING STARTED

I started training in the last week before my fortieth birthday by taking out membership of a local gym (the lovely Beech Club at the Westport Woods Hotel, County Mayo). There was a special offer for a three-month membership that was too good to miss and I liked the fact that it was for three months only, as when I joined, I wasn't sure I would even last a week. I was out of practice as regards exercise and had suffered sciatica and back pain in the previous years, brought on by successive pregnancies.

My goal was quite simple. I wanted to start exercising again and lose weight. I was totally out of condition and the only real exertion in my life was lifting small children and grocery bags.

I was a (part-time) working mother of four small children when I started going to the gym. The eldest, Nathan, was six years old, followed by Peter, almost five, Helen, three and Mary, 18 months. For my husband and I, managing our brood and day-to-day life and work was quite a juggling act and we were both in the market for some sort of outlet where we could let off steam and feel better about ourselves in the process.

As my fortieth birthday approached and it started to truly sink in with me that my body would never again be occupied by a growing baby, I experienced a wonderful new sense of self-belonging. This freedom was unfamiliar because I had spent six successive years either in the throes of pregnancy or recovering from giving birth and had rarely felt ownership of my body in that time. I had also felt very fragile for a long time after each birth.

I made the decision to explore my newfound sense of 'body-freedom' by doing something entirely for myself. I wanted to get back on track physically and shed the extra weight I had put on during pregnancy. Most of all, I wanted to be fit to run about after the kids and to look after them as well as could be.

So that's how it all started.

I wasn't a novice to exercise by any means when I took up running as I had once been quite a competitive young thing. From the ages of 12 to 21, I played squash at provincial level for Connaught and was even called for trials for the Irish team. I continued playing squash competitively when I went to university and played with the local Westport club right up until I became pregnant with our first child, at which point real exercise and sport vanished from my life.

By the time I decided to join the local gym, I'd been out of condition for at least ten years but was highly motivated to change that. I started by doing workouts on the various machines and I even had a motivational personal trainer whose advice I documented over the course of ten weeks in the form of a weekly log in my 'Wellbeing' column for the *Mayo News*.

After a few sessions of working out, I was happy to find I was enjoying it. I went to the gym two or three times a week and pushed myself hard enough, doing aerobic workouts for up to three-quarters of an hour. My personal trainer had bound me to keeping a food diary and I found this part more trying than the actual gym work, especially as I wasn't losing any weight. I decided to go it alone and worked out a fitness programme with the gym staff instead, promising to eat a healthy but unrestricted diet. I welcomed bread back into my life and began to look forward to my workouts.

My routine consisted of 15 minutes on the cross-trainer (Stairmaster), 10 minutes rowing and another 10-15 minutes walking on the treadmill. I only ever walked on the treadmill at first and never expected to run on it. After a while of regular gym attendance, I started to get a kick from the natural highs that followed these workouts. I also noticed small physical changes in that my clothes hung on me better and I could actually see the outline of my muscles hidden deep in my legs.

At the same time, I experienced a desire to push myself a little further each session, until the day it finally happened that I broke into a run on the treadmill. I used to walk fast for ten minutes or so, run for 2-3 minutes, then walk again. I found the running exhausting as I was carrying plenty of extra bits at the time and for a while, I did these short running sessions out of a sense of duty in my quest to challenge myself physically. The fact that I could turn on the TV monitor in front of the treadmill and distract myself from the task was an added bonus.

But then a strange thing happened. I developed a liking for the little bits of running and soon started to feel I wasn't doing a proper workout unless I ran for part of it. I even felt ready to up the ante a bit and consulted with John, one of the gym staff, who drew up a new fitness programme for me incorporating 'interval training'.

I was recommended to warm-up on the treadmill with a five-minute walk at a rate between 5-6km an hour, following which I was to run full whack (anything over 10km an hour) for one minute before returning to a jog for two minutes at 8-9km an hour. After the jog I had to run flat out again for another minute and over the course of 14 minutes, was supposed to do three of these interval series at a time.

The first time I finished the whole routine I thought I was surely going to die. My heart was pumping like a steam piston and my legs had turned to mush. It took an age for me to recover my breath and I don't know how I convinced myself to return and do it all over again a couple of days later. I left the gym hating it with a vengeance. John had also included weight-training and floor-exercises as part of my routine, which was set at 45 minutes.

After labouring at these workouts over a couple of weeks and literally talking myself through every minute of them, I acknowledged that I was genuinely enjoying them. Not only that, I had started looking forward to gym visits and was going to a lot of trouble fitting them into my schedule.

I was considering going back playing squash in the new year, instead of returning to the gym after my three-month membership expired, but then I noticed the interval training sessions were becoming much more manageable and that I had pushed my overall running time on the treadmill up to 30 minutes on one occasion. I read a story in our own newspaper about a 5k road race with a 'fun' category, which was to take place one week later, on St Stephen's Day. I decided there and then I would run that race. My mission was solely to run the 5k without stopping. In order to take part, I needed to train a bit longer and harder at the gym. I signed up for another three months.

Westport Athletic Club had been staging a 5km road race on an annual basis for years but I had never heeded it before. Because I had managed to run the equivalent distance on the treadmill in one go, I was pretty confident my body was up to running the 5k on the road too. I was therefore happy to mention to some people I knew that I intended participating and, out of the blue, my old squash partner Joan Staunton (Rowland), said she would come along too. I was delighted I wouldn't have to undertake the challenge alone and looked forward to enjoying Christmas and then getting it over with to run my big race!

Weather conditions on the day were perfect. It was cold but not too frosty and there was a lovely fog in the air. I arrived punctually at the sports complex to register and saw I was surrounded by athletic-looking people, all wearing top running gear, with some running on the spot and stretching themselves as part of a warm-up. I experienced my first nerves and felt jittery as self-doubt set in.

There was a problem, though, that nobody could pinpoint exactly where the start was. We all knew it was in the vicinity of the town library but not much else, and it took a further half-hour at least before the organisers picked the spot definitively. By that time, a pack of about 100 had gathered and as I clung to my body in an effort to stop it freezing over during the delay, a bunch of lithe individuals went running full laps of the Crescent, the residential area we were in. I seriously wondered whether I had it in me to do the run at all. Fortunately, I couldn't dwell on that thought too long as the gun finally went and we all moved off together as a pack.

Pure adrenaline kept me going as I was carried away by the novelty of all that was happening around me and the sensation that I was in a flow of movement. With my legs feeling like jelly, I rounded the first bend, to be greeted by my husband and our four little ones, whose eyes widened in surprise at seeing Mammy kitted out and running outdoors with this big ball of energy. Thrilled at the lovely show of support, I managed to keep running, albeit way too fast, until at last the route entered the private grounds of Westport House, which opened specially for the race. At last we were out of sight of the gazing public!

Joan and I were still together at this stage and she commented that I was going pretty fast and I agreed – too fast. I pulled in my horns and slowed down immediately, as I felt that after that first sprint I might not be able to continue at all. In fact, I was finding the reality of running outdoors very tough. Treadmill running was a cinch by comparison.

Joan was keeping an eye on her 11-year old son, Paul, who was running in the under-12 category, so she let me go on ahead and I found it a tremendous help knowing she was coming behind me all the way. My competitive spirit returned. I had to keep going in front!

By the time I managed to run the first mile or so of the race, I started meeting some of the long-legged male athletes – on their way back! I couldn't believe they could have completed the circuit already and thought maybe I didn't have much further to run after all. But they were true athletes running the race to improve on their times. They were basically sprinting the whole way and I subsequently learned that not only had they reached the gates on the other side of the estate but they had lapped the 'Pond' further along the way but we were all expected to do the same. So I just concentrated on putting one foot in front of the other and really appreciated all the good cheer wishes from race officials and passers-by, calling out 'Well done!' or 'Keep going, you're nearly there!'

A girl who had been running behind me then started catching up and we ran together for a while. She asked me how many races I had run, which threw me, as I felt I must have convinced her I was a runner of some sort. That gave me a terrific boost so I decided to keep going a while longer and the two of us ran side by side for a bit, until I told her to shoot on ahead if she wanted.

She sped up a little then and put some distance between us, but I found this even more helpful as I decided that no matter what, I would keep going behind her and finish the race in that order. And that is what I did. She kept going so I kept going. She ran up the little hill and down the final length and I followed her and came out the gates, where people were waiting to cheer us on again. I saw the finish line ahead and appreciated the words of encouragement sent my way.

I was curious enough at the end of all this to learn what my own finish time had been and asked, James, one of the officials for the information. He told me a little while later that I had come in at 'around the 30-minute mark'. I subsequently discovered he had been charitable in this assessment because in reality I must have been around the 40-minute mark, if not more. Still, it gave me a boost and new times to aim for in my training sessions on the treadmill.

Ernie Caffrey

With running, most people start at the bottom but I started at the top. My first competitive race was at the European Championships in Poland in the summer of 2006, at the age of 69, weeks after I had started training. All I ran in was the 60 metres. I had to run in the 65–70 years of age bracket and all the guys there were four or five years younger than me. I ran 16 seconds something, while those guys were doing it in 13, 14 or 15 seconds. It was all new to me but I've improved since with training.

I did run before, 50 years ago, but never competitively. I played football and did a bit of running back then but I wasn't focused and didn't take it up seriously, although I was quick enough at the time. I do have speed. I wouldn't be an endurance runner no matter what I tried. I don't have the make-up for it and wouldn't attempt to run a marathon.

The only time I really liked running was when I took it up this time. When you're a teenager, there are so many things to do and if you're not dedicated to any one thing, you're doing everything and you're good at nothing. That was me. I wasn't too interested in winning back then and wouldn't have been great on training either. So it was only when I really set myself some goals that I finally got down to proper training.

When I started back I was totally unfit. I was so bad I wouldn't walk. If I had to go to the post office, I'd drive a car. I would have found it hard to jog a hundred yards.

The first thing I wanted was to get down a bit of weight. I was two stone too heavy. I started by walking but before that, I went to the Mater Hospital in Dublin for a full medical check-up. Not that that's a guarantee, although it costs £500, but they said I was OK and to fire ahead. I intended pushing my heart rate up to maximum with speed training so you want to know it's not going to stop.

Then I got to like the running and it became competitive. I set a goal and one thing led to another. It was helping get the weight down and I started getting good at it.

In the beginning, I didn't want to go running down the track in case people would laugh at me – because of my weight and my age. So I got a quiet place out a walkway in Killala, where there was nothing except an old factory. I used to walk a bit, jog a bit and run a bit until I got a certain level of fitness. I graduated from there to the track.

I can well remember my first time at the track. All I could do was about 200 yards, but I gradually built it up to a mile without stopping. It didn't take me too long to do that.

I used to go down there in the dark at first so that people wouldn't see me. Then, during the winter I bought a treadmill and that was the real turning point. I put it beside the bedroom and could go on it any time I felt like it, day or night or when I got up in the morning. So the treadmill was really the key to getting fit because, with the weather being so bad, you couldn't get out at all.

Then I started doing sprinting and found the treadmill wasn't fast enough. I don't like watching the TV or listening to the radio when I'm on it. I like to be inside my own head. I was able to up the speed and get a buzz out of sprinting but the ordinary commercial treadmill will only do 10-12 miles per hour and that was no good for what I was aiming for.

So I built myself a super treadmill. I designed it and got a fellow to build it for me. I set it to do up to 20 miles an hour and I'm up to 15 on it now and it will actually go up to 25. It took four months to put it together but it's been fantastic. You have to get used to firing your legs faster or it's no good. I still go down to the track to get short bursts.

I never smoked, which is a big thing, but I did drink socially over the years. Before that I was a publican and, as you know, most publicans lead a sedentary life. They all have big bellies and are going nowhere slugging pints. I never saw a fit publican yet.

Grainne Cunningham

The first time I went running I was about 18 or 19. I was in America on my J1 Visa and bought a cheap pair of runners and went out a few times. I spent some time in England after that and occasionally went for walks that turned into runs.

But it wasn't really until 1996 that I started training for a mini-marathon in Cork. I wasn't running seriously, in that I didn't run through the winter. I thought if I could run for 30 minutes I was brilliant.

I remember finding some of the mini-marathons so hard. I did one in Dublin and, over time, five others, and always found them hard. Now I like them as a nice run. I would do a mini-marathon as an ordinary training run now and come home afterwards and be fine.

I don't think I am a naturally good runner. I see other people start after me and they seem to achieve faster times sooner and not get injuries, whereas I get quite a few. Sometimes I think why can't I be better but really, I think, can't you enjoy it? Even if you get competitive you're still not going to be that good because you'll always be an amateur anyway.

So I'm not an exceptional runner, just a real plodder. All I do is try to be consistent. I hardly ever get the speed training in. On my runs, I say 'shut up' to the negative voices in my head urging me to stop. I tell myself, 'Think positive, notice is it slightly uphill. Right, that's why you're struggling. Just keep going.' One of my rules is that I don't stop if it's an up because you will come to a down shortly and you'll be sorry you stopped.

I'm learning all the time, especially since I joined the Bray Runners Club. Before I was running mostly alone but getting a buzz from it. Since joining the club I've learned how little I know about running and how much more serious people are about it, even as amateurs. They change their diet and lifestyle to fit in with training.

Ray D'arcy

I came to running very late and by default, because what I really wanted was to learn how to swim. I attempted to learn to swim several times in my life and suddenly I was heading towards the big milestone of 40 years of age. I thought if it came to be that I had children (and now we have baby Kate), it would be embarrassing not to be able to swim with your kids.

I decided that this time I needed a really solid target because I had attended swimming lessons when I was in the Scouts and again in my twenties, but work or something always got in the way of persevering.

So in a moment of madness, on the radio – it was the day after the Dublin City Marathon 2003 – I said I want to learn how to swim so I'm going to do it as part of the triathlon next year in 2004, before my fortieth birthday.

The big thing there for me wasn't the running or the cycling but the swimming, because I had to go from not being able to swim at all to swimming a mile in the sea. I was already cycling a bit in and out of work, and to be honest I was also doing a little bit of running. There's a lap of around three miles around my home and every so often I would do that.

But I was never into running and could not see the appeal of it. The first pair of runners I bought was while on holidays down in west Cork. I remember going into Clonakilty for a pair. On the sand dunes along the coast in Inchadoney – any runners there will know this – there's a lovely, undulating lap. I reckon it's shy of a mile. Some football teams used to come there pre-season for stamina training, soccer teams from the UK. So that was one of my first runs. I did play team sports up to my thirties and throughout my thirties played five-a-side soccer, but that stopped and I felt I needed something else.

Mastering swimming was the huge thing for me and swimming in the sea on my own is the real challenge. I can't tread water. Tommy Tiernan describes it as 'having no neutral'. So I turn on my back and float. It's because I had to learn to swim and that was the priority. That took me so long I never had the luxury of learning how to tread water.

The guy who was training me had to achieve two things. Teach me how to swim and for me to be fit enough to swim a mile. He put me into flippers and got me up to 750 metres, around 30 lengths. I thought it would be nothing to take them off. That was July and when I did take the flippers off, it was like starting from scratch again. So I really only swam my first length at the end of July and then had to swim a mile the next month in the triathlon, which was tough.

But swimming is great. The first time I enjoyed it was after the triathlon because I got into the pool and had no target. I've neglected swimming since our baby, Kate, arrived; something has got to give. Because I was swimming twice or three times a week, running twice or three times a week and cycling in and out to work, it became impossible to maintain that level.

With running, I do eight-minute miles and that's it. I can't run any faster and I can't run any slower. I don't train with anybody. I happened upon that pace on my own.

Gerry Galvin
I started running in 1991 when I was 25 and living in England.The running started because of a squash coach who lived with us in London and who wanted us to do the 1992 London Marathon. There were a good few of my

colleagues in the squash club attempting it and the coach said if we trained for a year we would be ready for it. We trained, but not hard enough, and on the day it was really hard work.

I was always fit, having played hurling and soccer for years, and squash since 1988. The hurling finished because there were no referees in England and people there didn't have any idea how to hurl. If you were in any way good and ended up getting injured, you could be hobbling around, unable to work. I was 22 or 23 at that point and knew I wouldn't be going on to play in any great Croke Park matches

So that's where the squash came in. Both involved hand and eye coordination and squash fitted in well enough as a replacement sport. It was indoor, less physical, with less body contact or chance of getting injured, and very fast, so that all appealed to me.

It was pure coincidence that the squash coach, a South African guy, was involved in running.

The good thing was that England had better sports facilities than here. There was a Roger Bannister (the first athlete ever to do a four-minute mile) running club and six other harrier clubs where I lived. A lot of my running training was incorporated into my work. I worked in Bank in London and from Bank to Harrow was 18 miles. So on a Friday evening I used to run home from work for my long run in the week. Believe it or not, you'd only be half an hour longer than in a car, which would take one and a half hours.

Running is all in your head. If you're fit to run, fair enough, but how well you perform is a mental thing. As you're running you're thinking all the time about what's around the corner. It's a funny sport because it's so mentally intense. You can't wander, like with swimming, where you might think about what you're going to do the next day or something. But with running you've so much to think about, like the breathing, the legs, your arm movements, your hydration, how thirsty you're getting, the sweat coming into your eyes, whether you're chafing anywhere, are your runners hurting, is the sun in your eyes and all that. It's literally from your toes to the top of your head. You're cleaning out your nasal cavities as well, your throat cavities and all this mucus that builds up on your route, as it does. Then you might be thinking of having to go to the toilet. I found it more difficult when we moved to Westport im 1997 because of the lack of footpaths and lights. The motorists here had no great respect for runners and in the summer the problem is flies. There are lots of them here, whereas in England there were none. Sometimes when you're running, flies can interfere with your breathing. A fly in your eye could throw you out. Every little thing can throw you off.

Running requires every part of your body to move. Your head, your back, your neck, your bum, your legs: every part is being used to propel you along a road or up a hill. Your heart is beating at a constant rate, at a higher rate than in any other sport. In a marathon you're running for three and a half hours. There is no other sport where your heart will be kept beaing at such a rate, unless maybe if you're swimming the channel. So there's nothing compared to it.

In squash my heart rate is a maximum of 101 beats a minute whereas when I'm running, it's over 140. So that's the amount of pressure the body is under, the amount of energy that is needed, which is why such a high level of endorphins is secreted by the brain. They become like a drug because they provide such a feel-good factor.

Running isn't a very expensive sport. You don't have to join a particular club to become a runner. You can run on the road, the park, a hill, a sandpit. All you have to do is buy a pair of shorts, a pair of runners and get a bit of advice or maybe some coaching.

Everyone was born to run. All you need is to learn a bit about it, up your tempo and it will come. Watch also that you're not carrying a little bit too much extra weight.

Obviously you can spend money on good gear and all the energy drinks. In the marathon I used to take electrolyte drinks to replenish after the run but now I take purified water from a filter system installed in the house and it's as good. I don't drink any soft drinks and the kids are the same.

Mary Kennedy

I took up running in secondary school. I don't know why. I suppose you try everything in school and when you're good at something, you're encouraged. I must say our PE teacher was great. It was fun. Then I joined the Clondalkin Athletics Club, which was a small club but we did little bits here and there and I enjoyed the feeling of fitness and being part of the club.

When you're a teenager I don't think you look on it as a way to keep fit. I know my own kids are into sport but they do it more as a social thing and something to do after school.

I continued running when I went to UCD and in college it became more serious and more about fitness. Also you're part of a club then so you have to have that commitment, which I think is important. I always try to get my kids to have that same level of commitment. If they say, 'I don't feel like training,' or 'I trained too hard the last day,' my answer will be – 'Out with you.'

In UCD it was all short distances we ran but I was never really good. I got a few intervarsity medals but many of them were for second place or as part of a relay team. Still, it's nice to have the medals. It seems so long ago now.

The main reason I loved running was because the social life around it was second to none and that helped keep me involved.

Dr Mick Loftus

If I wasn't doing any exercise I would be inclined to be stout. Way back to my school days in Muredachs I was playing with the county at 18, having won a junior championship. I was on the Mayo minor team in 1947. That got me more involved in sport and it went on from there. I won three Sigersons Cup finals with UCG and at the same time I was involved with Mayo, playing two junior All-Irelands and a senior in 1951. So that involved a lot of training, although it wasn't as intense as it is now.

One day I was playing in a local seven-a-side here. I twisted my knee and tore the semi-lunar cartilage. Believe it or not at the same time I was house surgeon with the Orthopaedics Unit in Galway but they had no MRI scans then, just an X-ray, and couldn't do a lot with it.

From there on, if I twisted my knee playing football it would swell up, so I had to forego the football. I was at a game in Ballina one day and the referee didn't turn up so they asked me to do it. So I went from there to refereeing local games and eventually national events, junior and senior All-Irelands and the World Cup in America. Naturally for that I had to keep up my fitness, and running laps of the pitch didn't involve turning on my knee. But I never thought of it as I do now; I was never passionate about it.

In the 1960s I was very busy in my practice but was asked by the late GAA man, Johnny Mulvey, to go into administration. I was elected to the Connaught Council and went on to be the President of the GAA in 1985, '86 and '87. That's where my trouble with weight started, as between going out for meals and work, there wasn't time left over for much else. After my presidential years I was more than 15 stone, which was far too heavy, and I said to myself, I have to do something about this. I was about 60 years old.

I started walking and that's how I got into it. We had a nice route here in Crossmolina out and around Gortnor Abbey. It's a three-mile loop and you're on the road the whole time, but off the main thoroughfare. Then the odd time I'd maybe run five or six yards and I gradually increased it until I could run non-stop for the three miles. That was the challenge I set myself. I kept it up and gradually got into it after that. Maybe not too intensely at the start but over time I did more and more until I got to the point where I am now, where I run the three miles five out of seven nights a week. I would think running is advisable for everybody. I was quite heavy when I took it up. You start by walking and gradually run short distances and increase it that way.

Even if it's raining you have to go out. People ask me how I don't get colds but people have this idea that they need a lot of clothes on them all the time. I go around, I get wet and then have a shower. I don't remember being ill. So many go around bundled up in clothes but if they'd only take exercise they wouldn't need half as many clothes. Instead what they do is wear more and more and more.

I work from 10am through until 6pm here in the surgery every day and then I go home and tog out at about 7 each night. On the way back I call into my son, Michael's house. He has weights there, so I would do that each night and then have a shower. Honestly, I feel like a new man after it.

I have had a pacemaker in for the last dozen years because I have a slow pulse rate and the cardiologist advised it. The other thing is the arthritis which is in my knee, the one I injured way back. I went to see one of the orthopaedic fellows but I wasn't inclined to get anything done with it. I never plan to get anything done with it. I run away on it. I used to do another run here over hills for six miles. It's a route out the Castlebar road.

You hear them saying to rest the knee and take medication. I do neither. I keep going. Would I advise my patients to do the same? Well that's the thing. What I say is, well, I run on my knee and yes, while I might have a slight pain with it, once I run 30 or 40 yards and heat up, I forget about it.

Professor Risteárd Mulcahy
I got into running because I had been very sedentary up to the age of about 39 and then I was fortunate that somebody introduced me to the game of squash. I suppose I'm a little bit obsessional about things,

and I became a madly enthusiastic squash player. It brought to me the sudden realisation that physical fitness leads to mental fitness and to an extraordinary increase in one's self-esteem. For the first time I became conscious of the functions of my body and began to enjoy the physical exertion and exhaustion associated with squash.

I'd play four or five times a week, for an hour, which is quite a lot. I became very fit and active and got it down to a low handicap. Then when I was 50 I was playing very tough squash in Fitzwilliam although it was a game that people gave up at about the age of 30 back then. A number of other players and I began to introduce squash to middle-aged people. Although I stopped squash at the age of 50, some of my friends went on playing right up to their seventies. The reason I stopped was because I was so compulsive about it. If I had a really tough match I'd be exhausted.

I did row in UCD as a student and rowing was a great reminder to me of what a wonderful thing extreme exercise can be for you. The trouble about rowing is you're with seven or eight other people, you're in a race one-and-a-half miles long and it's all out from the beginning. So by the time you're half-way down the course you're exhausted but you have to continue because if you don't, if you stop, the whole boat will collapse. At the end of a race we would fall and actually collapse in the boat. On the Liffey you were often near a weir and if you weren't careful you could go over. Some of the oarsmen actually got sick with exertion. So we learned the hardship and also the fulfilment of extreme physical exercise.

On one occasion in my fifties I was playing squash with a person at my own level and we played five sets that all went to a tie-break. We both pushed ourselves to the limit and it occurred to me that maybe at that age I ought to reduce the intensity of my squash or give it up. I realised I couldn't reduce the intensity and noted that some of my friends had given up squash and were now running. I was intrigued by this and started myself, simply by walking around the tennis courts for 12 minutes. Then every day I would try and go a bit further so that after a few months I was doing a kind of power-walking, what I call jog-walking. In other words I would jog for 50 steps and walk for 50 steps. It took me about a year to convince myself I was capable of running, because being fit at squash is different from being fit at running.

The first thing that happens to people who take up running is they think they're not able to run because they're not designed by the Good Lord to run. Of course the problem is that they're not fit for running. About a year after I started out I suddenly got into a state of fitness for running and it was then I took up long-distance running, rather than sprinting.

I had many doubts for the first year or so and wanted to give up once or twice. You must realise you have to become fit to run and that is a slow process. If you try to hit it too hard you will run into trouble. That's what happened to me. I went to Phoenix Park and being impatient about my running, I ran for 20 minutes and at the end of that decided to give it up, because it was too hard. But a few days later I said I'd try again.

Mary Walsh

I was always active in team sports and loved them in school. I played camogie in college and did a bit of running then. I started travelling about after I graduated and that's when I really started running. It suited me because while you can be part of a running group if you like, you're not tied down. You go when you go.

I ran through my travels, in Australia, New Zealand and during my time in Armenia in 1989 when I was doing voluntary work with the Red Cross and Calcutta Rescue. I used to run in the mornings, right by the KGB office. It was the first time the Soviet Union allowed any foreign aid into the country. They had files on us and knew who we were.

I like going to new countries and taking runs early in the morning when you can see the place differently as it wakes up. I don't run in Muslim countries because as a woman you can't be seen in shorts and a t-shirt. I respect that, but I would go for walks instead.

I worked in Calcutta and walked 115 minutes to work each day. I did voluntary work twice, in Calcutta and Armenia. I wanted to see the world and help people. I also liked the concept of development work.

Running became more serious for me when I was in Canada. I lived there for a few years between the ages of 27 and 30, and did some triathlons, which included 10k runs. Then I came back home and worked as a physiotherapist with many teams training for major events. I couldn't commit to team sports as I would have liked, so running was fantastic. I would run a half-marathon in the morning or go to the gym. It was my escape.

I much prefer running outside and only do the gym if I absolutely have to. I'd say I've used it once in the last three years here in Westport and that's because it was so windy outside. I did a half-marathon on the treadmill and afterwards, for the first time ever, had a sore hamstring. Luckily, there is always somebody from my own profession there to help if I get injured.

2

Getting Hooked

The 5km race had a huge effect on me, not least the fact that my muscles were sore and stiff for days after. But most of all, I came away from it feeling at one with myself and the world and knew I had rediscovered the joys of demanding exercise. I had to take it further by continuing to push myself. I had excelled at one sport before and there was no reason I couldn't work hard at another one. I liked the idea of getting involved in running as really it was a new sport to me. My ambition was to be able to keep going and increase my distances, which I believed I could do. Stamina had always been my strong point, speed my weak point.

Marathons mesmerised me but the notion of actually running one for real was unreal. I didn't know whether I could even sustain my interest in running at this point, never mind my energies to keep going. But I did like the idea of exploring the notion of pushing myself and was up for a new adventure in my life.

Instead of deciding I would definitely train for a marathon (the most likely one being the Dublin marathon in October, 10 months away), I opted instead to look at the smaller picture and take things one step at a time. I vaguely remembered a 10km road race staged somewhere in Mayo the previous summer and thought I should aim to run that next summer. If I succeeded at that, I could aim for bigger things.

So that is how I approached my training. My goal was to up my running distances gradually with a view to eventually being able to run for 10 km. That, at least, was what was going on in my head. In my body though, a different story was at play. It was still in recovery mode from the 5km run and needed time to adjust to taking on such excursions on a regular basis. I was also very wary of overdoing it as I didn't want to end up with an injury of some kind.

For a while, I opted to work out every second or third day and concentrated on keeping going and staying active. Some time later I managed once more to keep running on the treadmill for 30 minutes, covering over three miles – around the equivalent of my 5km run. I decided this would be the minimum distance I would run on the treadmill from then on, and got myself to the point where I was completing a 5km treadmill run two or three times a week. And then it hit me. I needed to be outside again. I needed to run outdoors.

One Sunday morning, instead of going to the gym, I decided to head for the hills. At 9am, when it was still quiet, I took myself into town, and re-ran as much as I could of the 5km route that wasn't closed off. I ran for 20 minutes and found it a completely different experience from running on the treadmill. Running outdoors is the real thing. It's much harder work because you have to deal with the elements and naturally hilly terrain. Even if you choose to distract yourself by listening to music through a set of earplugs, the most powerful sound you'll hear will always be your own inner voice, constantly urging you to keep going (or maybe tempting you to stop).

I can't say I took much note on my run of the the beautiful coastline or green fields around me, as I didn't want to lift my head unless I absolutely had to.

I must mention at this stage that physically I was by no means a long lean running machine. On the contrary, I started off this running lark as a 5ft 7in, solid 12-stone woman. Although I did shed a full 20lbs in the space of the following eighteen months, unfortunately that didn't come about solely as a result of my new exercise regime.

The twenty-minute outdoor run took a nice bit out of me and I knew I needed to up my fitness levels overall by doing much more exercise in general. While all this was going on, my husband Padraic was getting in on the act. We started meeting people through the gym and built up respect for those who believed in training and exercising their bodies.

I was beginning to discover the truth about exercise: the more energy you use, the more energy you have to do other things. Every time I pushed myself physically, it seemed to fire me up to challenge myself even further the next time.

I decided I needed to start reading up on what I was learning and set about finding material on the subject of training and fitness. *The Irish Runner* and *Runner's World* magazines provided excellent information every couple of weeks but I also wanted to read entire books on the subject.

Our local Westport library, although small, is well stocked, and I loved going there on a regular basis. I looked for references to do with running but found very little on the subject. I asked the librarian, Keith, to do a search for me and he came up with four titles, which I asked him to order. Meanwhile, I went in search of further material in local bookshops.

I was surprised to discover that material on running, in the form I was looking for, was not readily available. I wasn't interested as much in running and speed techniques as in anecdotal accounts about people like myself, who had taken up running as adults and discovered the joys of it – and then I wanted to know what lengths they had taken it to. I was looking for ideas and inspiration about what I could do with this newfound passion of mine.

One specialist fitness magazine I came across (*Ultra-fit*) carried some excellent material on the subject, including an article, 'How to train for a marathon in six months'. Still very much a novice runner at this stage, I was heartened to read this but didn't feel any urgency about committing to doing one myself. I did, however, start taking note of the exercise I was doing each week and exactly what mileage I was covering over the seven-day period.

Over the first week in the New Year, I ran five miles. That rose to seven over the second week, when to my satisfaction, I completed a 3.5 mile run around a popular walking circuit with lots of hills (the Cloona walk). Hill-running was completely new to me and doubly so to my poor muscles. While I wanted to keep challenging myself further, I also felt a need to learn how to look after my muscles properly and not harm them in any way.

The marathon-training article advised that you should build up to running 10 miles a week before you even consider working towards a big race, so that distance was the focus for my training.

But I needed to understand how to recover properly from exercise and all about muscle stretching and flexibility, which I read were crucial elements of a proper training programme. I had never bothered being cautious about these issues when I was younger but I knew this time around I had to heed all the relevant advice, as my body had definitely changed and was heavier and much less flexible.

In regard to recovery, I learned that after each hard workout, I should give my muscles a day to recover and treat these days as 'rest days'. That didn't necessarily mean putting my feet up and eating anything I wanted but instead that I should remain active within the confines of normal movement and maybe do some floor-exercises or weight-training, using parts of my body not affected by the running. Once my fitness levels rose a bit, I could introduce cross-training sessions on the days in between running, which could consist of playing a game of squash or tennis or working out on some gym equipment or with weights.

While all this was going on, management at the gym were waiting for new treadmills to come in to replace old ones that had been removed. This went on for a while and bothered some people but my reaction to it was that I had to put my runs outdoors on a much more serious footing. After the few good runs I had had in the clean, fresh air, I knew that running would be real for me only when I did it outside.

For whatever reason, I was gripped by running to the point where – in the space of a couple of months – it had become an integral part of my life. It was a new thing for me to think about and was pretty much consuming my thinking during my spare time. I was constantly planning and working out ways to fit running into my life so that by the end of each week I would have clocked up a satisfactory number of miles.

The best part was that I didn't doubt my running capabilities any more. The treadmill training had been a huge help and I was so grateful that my knees, ankles and legs in general seemed to have no difficulty with running as an exercise. I remember one day around that time on the treadmill, as I was running at an easy pace, I suddenly felt that my legs could keep going like that forever. I looked down at my legs and told them to keep on going. It was a breakthrough moment and one that has stood to me ever since. Whenever I'm out for a run, I give myself the same message now. 'Keep going. You can do it.'

By the third week in January, I had started my running programme in earnest, both psychologically and physically. I was amazed to discover that in the space of three weeks, I had increased my stamina to the point where I could run the equivalent of my landmark 5km race on every second or third day, needing very little time to recover in between. Because I wanted my runs to be interesting and varied, I figured out the geography of my local area to work out good running routes. I also committed to investing in some good running gear to help me on my way.

Part of Westport is situated along the coast, and invariably I found myself drawn to that side where there are plenty of options for road running. I decided to add new stretches to the runs once a week, which would give me the recommended weekly 'long run'.

Up to that point, I had been calculating my efforts by the time I spent running, with 30 minutes being my cut-off point. I dearly wanted to increase my time and decided, for the second run in my third week of training, to add on a little bit. It took only another 10 minutes to cover the ground involved but the additional exertion proved hugely challenging. I really felt it in my limbs afterwards, as much as after my first 5k race.

As well as finding the slog involved tough going, I remained incredulous that I was actually out there doing this thing. How had I suddenly become a runner at 40 years of age?

I delved into further reading material on the subject that answered many of the questions popping up in my head. My find to date was an excellent book entitled *Improving with Age* by Irish cardiologist, Risteárd Mulcahy, who developed a love for running in his fifties and went on to run his first marathon at the age of 60. What an inspiration. I devoured his entire story in one night and found myself relating to a great deal of the contents. The author espoused running as probably the best all-round sport that allowed communion between mind and body. He recommended exercise in general to everybody as a means of adding on life years and wondered why an exercise culture for young and old was not heavily promoted by governments and health organisations.

He wrote about a map of the world he kept and a log of all the runs he had done in different countries across the globe. I had often dreamed of travelling the world but had never thought of running it. Another goal to aim for.

He also made many interesting points, such as the fact that the body will ensure it gets a good diet as fuel when training and won't tolerate overeating. I was already finding that to be the case, as my eating habits were changing. I preferred eating small, regular meals and enjoyed sating my appetite, rather than ending up feeling too full.

I felt reassured after reading this material. The fact that it had been written by a heart physician, in his eighties, who still did aerobic training and was so passionate about the benefits of exercise, won me over completely. Later on I was thrilled to meet Professor Mulcahy in the flesh when I was writing this book.

So I no longer doubted the path I was taking. Good health prevailing and injuries aside, I would continue regular running on a schedule of three to four times a week. I had a half-marathon in mind by then and had work to do, not least of all drawing up a timetable for running that wouldn't interfere too much with family life.

Running soon taught me what a wonderful thing fatigue is – exercise-induced fatigue. I had unwittingly experienced my first proper fatigue after the 5km road run, which put me beyond my limits at that time. But following my extra-long run in the third week of January, I experienced it again and fell in love with the feeling. It's good fatigue, brought on by exertion, as opposed to bad fatigue, which can follow periods of lethargy and listlessness. It makes you want to go out and work yourself up into the same state again, except you know instinctively – and your body tells you – that you need first to rest and recover.

During my recovery, I always felt great. While my muscles were tired, my body temperature would remain nice and high (helping to boost my immune system) and emotionally I would feel totally upbeat. It would be a case of waiting for my recovery to be complete before I could take off and push myself again.

From what I had read about the science of running to this point, I knew I had to be careful about pushing myself too hard too soon. I felt such satisfaction with what I had achieved in the space of my first few weeks that I decided to keep at this level for a while longer.

Unfortunately, two days after my long run, I discovered that my left ankle was swollen. I hadn't noticed it happening and couldn't remember having turned on it or hurt it in any way. But when I put all my weight on it it really hurt. I couldn't believe it. I was getting into my stride and was itching to keep at it. But I knew I wouldn't be able to run on the ankle and would have to get it checked out. I was sure rest would be recommended, and it was.

While he could diagnose no specific injury, Donal, an excellent sports massage therapist, told me he reckoned I had suffered some ligament damage. I started thinking back to my competitive squash days and remembering all the times I came down badly on my feet or hurt my ankles. I didn't remember ever having my injuries treated properly; instead I just hobbled through the pain.

This time around I decided I had to look after my body better. I wasn't in my twenties any more. I was recommended to rest my ankle for five days and I made a decision not to do any outdoor runs during that time. However, I simply couldn't stop running altogether. I felt I'd been building up to something with all the hard work I'd already put in and found it impossible to let that go. I feared if I gave up running then, I would never get back to it again. By then I loved everything that went with the sport: the highs, the lows and the constant challenges. So I followed the advice regarding the RICE code, which recommends rest, ice, compression and elevation for injuries, but finding the Rest part difficult to stick to, continued running on the treadmill. I knew I should have stopped altogether because it certainly hurt to run, but after ten minutes or so, I found I was able to work through the pain.

On alternate days I rested and then ran, but was devastated that I couldn't run outdoors and increase my time. I was also growing increasingly worried about my ankle's slow recovery. I had by now developed a habit of turning my foot to minimise the impact on my ankle.

My recovery, when it did come, was worth waiting for, although of course I know it would have come quicker had I not run at all. I was also lucky I didn't do any permanent damage to my ankle, having refused to rest it altogether.

At any rate, two weeks later, the pain eased off. I felt well enough to push myself again and so I did, running my longest ever non-stop on the treadmill for an hour at an average 9km speed, burning up over 700 calories and covering more than 8km in the process. It was a good workout and I enjoyed the buzz afterwards. Still, I knew it didn't compare to the real thing outdoors.

Another two days later, feeling sufficiently recovered, I prepared to run in the open air. I was actually nervous about hitting the road for the first time in a fortnight. The route I had opted for was the 3.5 mile Cloona loop, which involves some serious hills but also carries the fabulous reward of a long downhill run to the finish. I had run it once before and nearly died after it. This time, I felt my fitness levels should have improved enough to make it that bit easier.

It was a beautiful Sunday, early afternoon. The air was cool and foggy, the road dry and hard. I started slowly, finding it tough to keep going in the outdoors again. I even doubted myself and thought of stopping. But ten minutes into the run, I got my second wind. I scaled the first hill and came down the other side feeling wonderful. It was so easy when I knew the route and where exactly to anticipate the hard bits.

When I got to the lovely, drawn-out final downhill, I ran as though my life depended on it. I sprinted and sustained the sprint like I'd never done before. Speed was something I wouldn't ever have associated with myself but suddenly, I couldn't get enough of it. I pushed on and on, feeling totally exhilarated. My ankle felt good, my body movements flowed perfectly. I was the very best I could be at that moment in time. It really was the nicest feeling in the world.

The run lasted for 30 minutes but the after-effects kept me going all night and again the next day. I was so thrilled to have got out there once more, so grateful that my body had forgiven me for whatever damage I had done to it and relieved that I hadn't lost my confidence to run.

By then, I knew what stretches to do as part of a proper cooldown and promised to do them after every run. I also decided not to push myself too hard, too soon, and opted to continue with my three runs a week – two of three miles and one of four miles. I kept this going for the next few weeks and felt on top of the world, anticipating the moment when I would feel my fitness levels moving up another notch.

By the way, at this stage I had also lost half a stone and my clothes were getting loose on me. Big advantage.

My next training session some days later took me back indoors to the gym where I stayed running on the treadmill for 60 minutes. Again this hour-long workout, which I managed once more at a 9km pace without too much trouble, gave me a real taste for the marathon running I was considering working towards.

I started thinking about this and wondering was it really feasible. Could I really keep my body going for such a long time in the sustained exertion of running? I wasn't sure I could. I definitely needed to build up gradually before I could fully absorb exactly what was entailed in such an enormous challenge.

I had also discovered another book by an excellent author, British woman Sam Murphy, in her book *Run for Life*. It was written specifically for women interested in the sport and backed up everything I had been feeling in terms of the highs that go with regular running as well as giving lashings of information on how to train properly.

However, almost two months into my 'training' and still wired by my ever-increasing love for running, I had to endure a period of sheer frustration. Although I had convinced myself that my ankle had recovered from whatever strange injury had previously ailed it, I was forced to admit it had been a case of mind over matter. My recovery was a myth.

I happened to be staying overnight in a beautiful hotel in County Sligo, the Radisson SAS, as part of a review I was writing up on the spa there. The hotel was located about three miles from a popular beach at Rosses Point and I determined to do the run up to it first thing in the morning. It was along a big, wide, national road – a type I hadn't had much experience on. I kept going for 40 minutes, which was good enough for me, and then jumped into the hotel pool, followed by a hissing steam-room session and a dip in the outdoor hot tub. I deserved it all.

Sadly, it was following this outing that the tenderness in my ankle returned. I had to grit my teeth and run through pain for up to ten minutes before I felt a breakthrough in running sessions after that.

Once more, I couldn't bear the thought of not being able to run, even for another week. I was so hooked on running by then I practically lived in fear of having it taken away from me. It's hard to explain because it sounds so irrational, but I think running can make you irrational. It really can hit you like a drug and have you craving for it and thinking about it all the time.

So again I did exactly what I shouldn't have done and persevered through the pain a few more times. Eventually, my entire left leg went into a spasm every time I ran on it. I could walk on it OK but if I dared even jog on the spot, the pressure immediately became too much.

There was nothing for it but to accept that rest was needed. I had to stop running – this time long enough to let a full recovery take place. Absolute torture. I knew already that even taking two-day recovery breaks could put you off your stride. I had been sticking to running every second day and balked at having to cut back again or cut running out entirely. I was really afraid I would lose the ability to do something that had become such a joy in my life.

All was not lost in that I continued going to the gym and worked out on low-impact machines. In fact, I had forgotten how good a workout the equipment could give and found the buzz from sessions on the cross-trainer, bicycle and rowing machine pretty good. I was grateful to be able to do that much in the knowledge that I hadn't done myself some serious injury. I didn't know what exactly was wrong with my ankle but whatever it was, I couldn't wait to have a clean bill of health again. I was itching to get out and run.

Ernie Caffrey

I always had a poor digestive system but that cleared up with the exercise. As I got older I was having more digestive trouble. Doctors said it was something I'd have to live with, that it was part of my inheritance. I remember hearing my father talk about his stomach so my problem was something similar to his.

When I started racing initially, my problem was I was rather slow getting out of the blocks, so I worked on that. It's the first 30 or 40 feet that are the slowest because you're taking off. I am fast and I have great flexibility as well. I never lost it over the years and it has stood to me.

My time is still improving instead of going down – whatever length that will last. In the competitions people were usually five years younger than me – at 65 when I was 69 – but I was keeping up with them, so it didn't bother me. Now I'm one of the younger ones in the 70-75 age category.

My first big win was in my second competition, the indoor All-Ireland Masters' Championship in Nenagh in January 2006. I won the 60-metre dash in 9.3 seconds. At the race I had nine grand-children shouting for me. One of them has taken up running since.

I'm running the World Championship in Italy in September in the 100m and 200m. I'm looking forward to that and to taking a few weeks' holiday there too.

I train on the treadmill 80% of the time because you can gauge exactly what you're doing with regard to time and speed and everything. The other 20% would be on the track. I don't find training takes too much out of me provided I do it sensibly. Of course there is a lot of new ideas now about training, like everything else, but I find that a little often is the best practice. I don't go in for muscle-building or lifting weights. You run with your legs and that's it. The arm swing propels you too and must be in harmony with the feet. Your feet can't be going at 15mph and your arms at 10mph. You must synchronise.

Some people can't tolerate a treadmill but I like it for the purpose of speed. I would start at what I call a very fast walk, at about 8.5km an hour. I might do a mile of that and then do short bursts of high-intensity running. Maybe a minute as fast as I can travel, then a half a minute fast. Afterwards I do a bit of stretching.

If you vary the routine it's not as monotonous. I'd be very much into stretching, getting the hamstrings and things right, and that takes time as well. I also like to develop techniques in running, looking at how I hold my arms, lift the legs. Constant jogging can really slow you up because you're inclined to drag your feet over the ground so you're using less energy. When you're sprinting you have to lift them, hips high, lift the feet. It takes more effort but you develop a better technique. That's why I don't like too much jogging. I'd rather fast walking because you're moving your legs very quickly and you're stretching out, even though you're only walking.

I do about 30 minutes in the morning and if I feel like it in the evening, maybe another 30 minutes. I like to do a bit every day.

Grainne Cunningham

Running is great. It's really rewarding and powerful. I go through things in my head. I ask myself, running up a mountain: what am I doing? I could be sitting at home with a nice glass of wine and my husband beside me. Instead, I'm in a place where my lungs are burning, my calves are hurting. All I can see is the back of the legs of the person ahead of me. I don't even want to lift my head as it's too much effort. I lift my feet because that's what you do. It's gruelling but then the summit is there and you're doing a downhill.

I love running by the sea and do a lot of uphill and road running. As much as I can I will stay off the road but I also like to get in some hills and it's all climbing up Killiney Hill until you get to the park. I always run for 35-40 minutes and then on a weekend try to run for longer. If I was training for a marathon it would be much more intense.

I've also started to run with the Irish Mountain Running Association in Wicklow, which can be very hard. You end up running up mountains all the time with your lungs absolutely screaming at you. There could be 200 people out on the mountain on a Wednesday night. I often think if anyone came across us they wouldn't know what was happening. Cars parked in a field and then the realisation that there are 200 people going to run up a mountain.

Running on heather and turf is gorgeous because you bounce and when you are going downhill you don't have to worry about your knees. It's like a little trampoline. It's so beautiful to go up into the Wicklow mountains, to get up to Prince William's Seat and look at the view from the top, 360 degrees around. You see the sun so close like a big ball in the sky and all the great scenery.

I get such a buzz going downhill as I seem to be able to go fast. I can overtake guys whereas I never could on the way up. I think then I must be doing something right.

Overall, I'd say I run for fun. I love it. I like running with people very much. It's nice being part of a group. I love the buzz after a long run. It's like a drug and I know I get a kick out of it.

But I also run because I want to get away from family life – not to escape it but for my own space and time off from ordinary routines. Definitely another reason I run is to keep fit. There is no denying that is a big part of it. I find running really effective as a way to get fit and to stay fit.

I think because you are fit and continue running, it keeps you on track in that you don't drink too much or anything. You wouldn't want a hangover if you're running the next day. So you won't take that third glass of wine because you know you will feel it tomorrow.

The number one for me is the friendships and the relationships you have through running. Also, finishing a run is what's great, not starting it. You feel so good at the finish and that's what I look for.

I try to run three times a week. It has to be normally when I have cover for the kids so that gives me a run at the weekend when Simon is here, maybe another when we have a child-minder in the week and I take an hour out. Then some mornings I get up at 6.45 and run before Simon leaves for work. That's really hard, especially in the winter.

Ray D'arcy

Doing a triathlon means you have to be able to run 10k so in order to work up to this, I started running twice a week. I soon began to see the mental benefits of running and started to get a kick out of it. I suppose this happens to everyone once the initial drudgery passes.

I think the combination of getting the endorphins and feeling good about it and enjoying it all got me in on it. Then when I did the triathlon, I did a good 10k. It was 55 minutes, which is not good for a normal 10k, but in a triathlon it's good because the run comes at the end after you've swum a mile and done your 20-mile cycle.

So I kept the running up. I was doing the odd 10k, maybe once a month. Then Jenny and I signed up to do the West Cork half-marathon but she got pregnant so I ended up being embarassed into doing it. The most I had ever run was the 10k so I decided I'd better do a little bit more if I was to cover 13 miles. I ran what I thought was a circuit of three miles three times, but it turned out to be 3.5 miles so I had done over 10 miles and went on to actually enjoy the half-marathon and find it easy. I had loads in the tank and was able to run fast for the last mile or so. I love west Cork too and the route was great – from Glengarriff to Bantry. So I did it in a good enough time of 1 hour 40.

It's great when you're running because you concentrate on that. You listen to your body a lot, thinking, maybe I shouldn't be hurting now, or whatever. Last week it took me to six miles before I got any comfort in my run and then I got a pep in my step, which made the last four miles enjoyable. I don't listen to music or anything. Sometimes I come up with ideas. Last year I dreamt up all the ideas for sponsorship of my Dublin marathon effort while I was running. I hadn't done the triathlon for charity so I said I would run the marathon for charity. One idea was the text-in competition to guess my time. Everyone said for a man of my age, running a marathon for a first time, four hours would be a very good time, so I was happy to do it in 3 hours 41.

We also got 20 corporate sponsors who agreed to give me 5,000 euro for every minute less than four hours that it took me to complete it. So if I did it in 3 hours 40 I would get 100,000 euro. There was no way back then.

Before I knew it, I got pulled into this whole marathon thing and said in public that I would do it. I printed up a plan starting at 20 miles a week, building up to 40 miles, and had five months to work towards that.

It is hugely time-consuming training for a marathon because it's not the time it takes you to do the runs but once you start doing the big runs, you're wiped out for the rest of the day. So if you do a 20-mile run your day is gone really, because firstly, you have to eat two hours beforehand; then the run is going to take you 2 to 3 hours, after which you need to cool down and shower and then you're whacked. You can't do a 20-mile run and then go off as if you've done nothing.

Only when I did my first 20-mile run did I think, Jesus, if I can do that I can do the marathon. I had met loads of people at the triathlon who ran the Dublin marathon who said they would never go near the marathon again, it was that extreme. The triathlon is much easier, much more fun, with lots of variety. If you come home in the evening and it's raining you can go for a swim; you don't have to run. But with the marathon, it really is drudgery. You have to get out there and do the miles and keep doing the miles. You have to run.

I'm glad I rediscovered running. If I come home and Jenny and Kate aren't there, I'll go for a run. I do two laps regularly which take me 28 minutes each. I would like to do some more triathlons if I can get around to them.

Gerry Galvin

I run five days a week. Some people go to the pub, I go for a run. Maybe I'm sad, I don't know. It's been said to me Sunday nights are for drinking, but for me they're for running.

When you have the sport done, you think very clearly. You're sharper, more focused. You don't seem to be as forgetful or make silly mistakes. You check everything. Your subconscious mind seems to be working a lot better too. You remember to put things into kids' lunch-boxes for this and that. You don't have to write things down, such as to ring someone.

I remember Mondays were bad for me in terms of being inefficient. That would have been from maybe going out drinking one night and not running. I would do silly things with the machines, Now I'm all business and much more active.

I didn't give up after my first bad marathon experience because I found that running is the most addictive sport I've ever come across. I decided I would give maybe a half-marathon a try again, but after two weeks we were back out training for another marathon. We made some adjustments, got proper running gear and shoes. As you progress you improve on everything: wear lightweights, get rid of water bottles. You don't want to carry any extra weight on a marathon. No music for the race either as you don't want to be missing any announcements or anything else. You want to have all your faculties.

So you carry the bare necessities and shouldn't even have to wear a cap or gloves, unless it's the Moscow marathon or somewhere with very severe conditions, because they gather weight. There's no need for flappy jackets either because they catch the wind and the last thing you want is to do anything that prevents you from moving. So dress light. The more aerodynamic you are – it's like a car – the more efficiently you travel.

We built up to doing seven or eight half-marathons in the year and then one marathon. I used to look forward to all the different courses, the Bristol, the Maidenhead, the Reading. It's a lot to fit in over a year when you're working but I loved it. I did five half-marathons after the London marathon when I got involved with the Hyde Park Harriers. We used to train in Hyde Park every Saturday morning. It was superb. We did half-marathon or 15 mile routes around the park, lovely lawns, running paths and safe. I got to know other people out running and got involved in social events.

My wife Mary worked in Northwick Park children's hospital, part of St Thomas's Hospital. We ran some of the half-marathons for Great Ormond Street, which is probably the most prestigious children's hospital in the world. Their team really looks after you after the marathon with masseurs, special Portacabins and all the gear.

Now I totally rely on night-time training as with family and work commitments, I can't get out during the day. I like to do my long run on Sunday. To achieve a long run you need to have your head clear and even having a few drinks on Saturday night ruins everything. So I decided to give drink up for three or four months to get the winter out of the way but then I went off it altogether because I felt it was so beneficial. I decided if I was going to have a drink it would be after a marathon where I would be resting anyway or on a special occasion. But it hasn't got to the stage where I've become a pioneer.

Maybe age is a factor too because at 41 I'm not going to get fitter. I have to eliminate certain things in order to achieve a better standard. I'm a lot fitter than I was ten years ago though, even though I didn't really notice it happening. The running may have taken the sharpness off my squash a little as the body movements are different and the brain is programmed more for running. They always said about dual players that they were good one day in one game and good another day in the other but they were never good at the two on the one day.

I wouldn't play squash when I'm training for a marathon because it plays havoc with the muscles in my upper back. I think you're over-sensitive to any other sport or activity when you're getting fit for a marathon because everything is so fine-tuned for long-distance running. You're eating around it, you're sleeping, going to bed earlier, needing eight hours of good sleep a night.

I stick to a pretty healthy diet. For breakfast I have cereal, usually Special K, with strawberries and bananas for lots of fibre. Bananas play a huge part in my diet. Then I have two slices of high-fibre toast and tea. You have to cut out coffee because it is a diuretic and not recommended. I do have one cup of coffee a day because I don't drink and I don't smoke so that's the only way I can spoil myself. At around 10.30 I have fruit and yoghurt and then at lunchtime, I have a full dinner: potatoes, meat and vegtables. A good meal, end of story.

I don't eat again until 9pm, after my run. If I need something small bananas are my preferred snack, maybe with a cup of tea. After the run I have another bowl of cereal. At night I also have a handful of nuts and raisins, which are excellent as they have Omega 3 which oils your joints. It's all about getting fuel. Junk food wouldn't appeal to me.

On a Sunday I do spoil myself, let the hair down a bit; but I have my run in by then. So maybe a piece of carrot cake. I mean I'm pure amateur, not professional. I'm not getting paid for this. My discipline can only go so far. The drive comes back to this whole thing about the adrenaline and the rewards you get from the feel-good factor.

There are good days and bad days at everything but the bad ones won't turn me off runnng. It's like everything else. For every bad day you'll have at least two good days and you really only have bad days when you're not prepared or there have been some changes in your routine.

It's essential to have a full dinner because that fuel will stand to you. Our coach here, Gerry, said to eat like a pig at dinnertime. Eat well. Don't spare it. Get the meat in, the vegetables, the whole lot and it will stand to you once you get over the 10 or 12 miles.

Before I used to take an awful long time to get tuned in, warmed up on a Sunday. The second breath used to take an awful long time coming. I'd be switched on now much more quickly and second wind doesn't really come into it any more. When you're starting off in training it's very noticeable when you start to feel relaxed. But as time goes on you become relaxed very quickly so it's not an issue any more.

There's better oxygen at night and I find I'm ten times better. As the summer comes in and the nights get longer, it gets easier.

Mary Kennedy

When I left college I kept up running for my own sake but never joined a club again. I didn't really have any gaps from it, maybe the odd time I was having a baby.

There are times of the year when it's really very difficult to fit running in workwise. When I was doing *Open House* I generally fell off between September and January. It was the New Year when work became less pressurised. My work now is flexible with *Nationwide* and *Up for the Match*. I could be anywhere in the country. For instance, I got back from Sligo last night at 5.30pm and was out on my run by six. I was so stiff after being in the car for so long, I was dying to get out and ran for 40 minutes. Even when you do give it up for a while, you can get back into it easily enough. It takes about six weeks or so to build back up your levels of fitness. I never pushed myself really hard.

I've stuck with running for many reasons. I find it energises me. It makes me feel less tired than I might have done before going out running, and keeping at it makes me feel a bit better about myself.

I do think it gets harder as I get older but the sense of pushing yourself is good because you're moving outside your comfort zone. There is a sense of wellbeing and you feel more positive about life. You're less susceptible to getting down. It's about the levels of oxygen you are getting and when you feel fit you are more in control.

I must admit that running isn't necessarily my sport of choice. Sometimes I would rather clean toilets. But at times like that, I always remember Noel Carroll's advice, which was to keep running for six minutes anyway and by then you'll be prepared to keep going. Most of the time I have to say I don't go out running joyously. But if I see somebody out having a run, I often feel I would love to be out there too. It never bothers me if I've already got my run in that day myself.

By choice, I like to run in the mornings because it sets you up for the day. I go out three or four times a week. I don't do a lot but what I do keeps me going. If I'm going away for a long spell somewhere, I'll try and get the three runs in before I leave, maybe one day after the other. It's a lovely feeling to go away knowing you deserve to enjoy yourself.

Usually, I run from my front door and do about 30 minutes, unless I'm trying to build up for something. I love looking in gardens and houses when I'm running. Some runners have things in their ears and listen to music or the radio as they run but I love to get away from all that and think and breathe and smell. In the summertime everything is so nice. The air in Dublin isn't as bad as people think thanks to Mary Harney's no-smog policy.

I'm going to the Aran Islands for the weekend and will be running there. I love running down the country, especially in Kerry. I love the fact that you run out with a certain type of topography in the foreground, the mountains, lakes and things, then you turn around to run back again and you view everything from a completely different angle. I always go up and back and make sure that for the first half the wind is in my face so that I am entitled to have it easier on the way back. I also love if I am running along past queues of motorists trying to get on to the M50.

I run for my own fitness and of course to keep the weight down. I'm always trying to be half a stone lighter and more toned. It gives you permission to have the wine and food in the evening. I adore good food.

I don't think running is for everybody. An awful lot of people like walking. But it's got to the stage where it's part of my life.

I love the days when I don't have to run because it's a rest day. I suppose I'll keep at it until the knees cave in. Then maybe I'll have to take up something else when I'm older. I might try golf.

Dr Mick Loftus

My participation in the World Senior Games competitions came about as a result of my involvement with the National Council for Ageing and Older People. My colleague there, Mary, mentioned that the event in St George, Utah, was for over-55s. On my third annual visit there, in October 2006, (aged 77), I drew gold.

They started the Masters in St George 25 years ago for the very reason of getting older people active and maybe to promote their area at the same time. It's a Mormon town, out in the desert, very strict, although it's only 120 miles from Las Vegas, with a population of 25,000 people that has since risen to 120,000. They had 600 entrants the first year and 9,500 last year from 50 countries. The events are across all fields, from basketball, to tabletennis, archery and athletics. It was something special to participate in. Edie, my wife, and I were the only two from Ireland and we went in with the tricolour, naturally.

As we got to know people there we were amazed how interested they were in Ireland. Maybe we flew the flag and attracted people to Ireland in that sense. The Ethiopians, as we know, are great runners and their manager took me aside to offer some advice. He told me the laces in my runners were too long.

I came second in the 5,000-metre race in the 75-80 age group and the next day put my name down for the mile race, as competitors were allowed to enter four events. I went in to participate but you know, when you're out on the track, you give it everything. I didn't mean to win it because I had the 3,000 metre race three days after but I managed to win the 3,000 anyway. It all goes on five-year age groups so I suppose that made it a bit easier. I've two years left in that 75-80 category but the trouble now for me is that the next time round I'll be one of the older ones in it.

I was disappointed to have come second in the 5k because that was the one I was really interested in. But temperatures were up in the eighties there and in the seventies in the mornings when we ran. I was a minute or two behind the winner.

I am passionate about running at this stage. I've got into the habit of doing my runs in the evening. I'm down here at 8am for Mass, start work at 10am and the day can be hectic, like today, when I didn't get lunch until 2pm and then I had to go down the country to take a man's blood. But I find I can take the pressure from patients. I never find myself getting ratty with them, even though they say as you get older you get more annoyed with people.

I look forward to going out for the runs. Maybe it's an effort to get out there but you feel so good after it when you come in and have a shower. And healthwise, I've had no problems from the arthritis or the pacemaker. Running helps you very much with your thinking and your concentration. I am into the Alzheimers age-group and I know that exercise slows down the onset of conditions like these. From a woman's point of view, exercise is one of the best things to prevent osteoporosis. It's good for the mind because it keeps it active and it also stimulates the circulation.

It's a pity a lot of young people don't keep up the exercise they do in their youth. If they could only keep it up in their thirties and forties, which is when 90% of footballers stop training.

If I suffered an injury that meant I couldn't run again I feel I'd be doing weights or you'd see me sitting into a machine. It's my lifestyle now and I enjoy it.

You do have to make time for running but you can if you want to. I manage it between meetings and work and all the committees I'm involved in. [Among other things, Dr Loftus is Chairman of Crossmolina Community Council, Vice-President of the Connaught Council GAA, a member of the board of management of St Muredach's College, Ballina, a member of the National Council for Ageing and Older people and a member of the Green and Red Fund, a local charity).

I was always involved in the community and with four children, I was fairly involved with the family too. I suppose the fact I wasn't drinking or on sessions at weekends left me with more time. We were never into that scene of going out for dinner or whatever at weekends.

My feeling on alcohol is that it is all about self-discipline. If people could avoid it they would be fine. Even young fellows out for the weekends, not necessarily drinking that much, still cannot work properly on the Monday. They haven't the go in them. Healthwise there's no other substance that causes so many illnesses from head to toe.

I never drank. It was probably football that kept me away from it and the Pioneers were fairly strong when I was growing up. We were 18 when we played in the minor All-Ireland and everyone was a Pioneer. The culture of alcohol wasn't there. We didn't have that pressure young people do nowadays.

The drinks industry is promoting this culture and that's part of it. If you're not drinking, you're an outsider. It's a very subtle way they promote it but the amount of money they can put into those ads is something else. And then at the bottom you have 'Enjoy alcohol responsibly'. It's so laughable.

What I think is wrong is that people are not taking enough responsibility for their own health. They go to hospitals complaining this is wrong and that is wrong when they should in a certain way be responsible for their health by exercise and good diet. They don't need equipment or anything else. Just a good pair of shoes, a pair of sneakers.

Here in the west of Ireland look at the lovely routes we have to enjoy. The odd time I go down to the beach in Enniscrone and jog up and down. It's the best part of four miles. But last Monday I happened to be down there, a lovely beach on a lovely day, and there weren't 20 people on it. I think if I was living in Enniscrone I'd be running that beach every day.

Professor Risteárd Mulcahy

I used to go out on lovely warm Saturday and Sunday mornings when nobody else was around and run alongside the Sandymount Nature Reserve. I would run and go into an almost dream-like contemplative state seeing the distant hills, the blue sky and no sign of life. It was wonderful. That's why it's so important you run in places that are nice and safe where you feel you can commune with nature, with God. It's a substitute for prayer really. That's what it meant to me.

I can get that feeling now through walking. It's more difficult but walking is a good substitute and is also very rewarding and can be contemplative enough.

So running is very rewarding and good for you mentally. You're very conscious of the circumstances under which you're running, whether it's a nice area, a quiet area, if it's warm or cool. You don't have too many clothes on – light shorts, good proper shoes – the sun is shining, and you're out there in the middle of nature. The type of impact you get from running or walking leads to the addictive element of it. What happened to me was that I became addicted to running. Now I'm addicted to walking.

The way you measure addiction is how do you feel when you've stopped it for a day or two. Let's say you walk six days a week and you miss it for two or three days, then you get anxious. It's a type of withdrawal effect.

I first discovered this many years ago when we started doing research work on heart patients. We discovered doctors were making heart patients stay in bed and stop taking exercise. We reversed that completely. We set up a system with post-coronary patients, recovered from heart attacks, whereby we got them to walk three miles every day, except maybe one day a week. A lot of people latched on to this – not everybody – but with persuasion on our part we got people involved. When they came back once a year for us to see how they were getting on I would ask them how they were doing with their walking and they would say, 'Oh I never miss my walking. I couldn't miss it now.' So they became addicted to walking.

Having experienced extreme physical exercise and the effects it had on me gave me an advantage when I took up running in later life. I can describe that exactly to a person who might like to take up exercise. People come in here to me for stress tests. I put them on the treadmill and we push them to the limit. Most of them take no exercise so I usually give them a talk then on the benefits of exercise and how to go about it.

A good fit person can run for up to 14-15 minutes in the stress test. The treadmill increases its elevation and speed every three minutes so it's pushing them really hard. Others can't do that of course. They may stop after a few minutes. It starts at 1.8 miles per hour and goes up to 4mph, but that's with the incline raised as if going up a steep hill.

Mary Walsh

Overall I get a buzz from running. I love the sociability of running with others but love having space on my own too. Your head empties because you are thinking of your body. When you are training properly, you eat properly. If I don't eat properly and then go running I feel awful.

I have a fairly good diet. I eat stuff that suits me. I don't eat meat but I eat chocolate and I drink. I don't like tea or coffee.

You can eat anything you want and still lose weight when you're training so that is something I love about marathons. I eat my normal food but that isn't enough. You have to reward yourself. You're asking a lot of your body.

My body feels so good when I am running. I cannot imagine not doing it. The older I get the more important running is to me. I rarely do it seriously now, as in training for a marathon. My aim now is to minimise the stress on the body. I prefer to run for fun and not to beat my times or anyone else any more. I'm happy to be able to keep running as I get older.

It's no surprise that I'm sporty. My dad was always really active. He played rugby and soccer for Connaught and the whole family was always big into sport. On Sundays we were always off at some match or other

I always run in the morning if I can. I need activity, whether it's hill-walking, squash, cycling or swimming. It keeps me sane. My number one passion is running but I also like walking up hills and mountains.

I'm in Mayo Mountain Rescue and I remember one day after doing an 18-mile run being called up the Reek [Croagh Patrick, 2,510 feet high] to help lift down a casualty. It was good recovery training.

By nature I was always a sprinter. I was fast. I also did the long-jump in school. I was only mediocre but they were my things. I loved playing on the wing at camogie too because you had to run against people out for the ball and I would always beat them.

There are times I don't run for a week or two. I'm not fanatical about it but I like doing things like half-marathons because it focuses you again. I like to settle into the run.

To reduce the toll on the body I like to run on grass or on the beach when the tide is out. Bertra beach near Westport is lovely for that. I run around the whole island. You feel so alive when you've been out there in all the elements.

There are some people who would rather not run. There is no point if you don't enjoy it because you are more likely to give it up. I don't think it matters what activity people do as long as they are exercising, because it's all good for you – your muscles, joints, bones, in combating obesity, osteoarthritis and ensuring good health. It's most important for children aged 11-18 to be active when the bone is really laid down.

In the last five years or so there has been a real increase in people running. With Croí [the Irish Heart Foundation] we've seen it. In the 2001 charity marathon there were 14 participants in the group, whereas last year 80 signed up for New York.

Everybody is built differently and moves uniquely. You should be using your arms, your upper body, your trunk, you whole body to run, not just your legs. Your stride should be even and whatever length is comfortable for you. It's important that you warm up and cool down. For those of us who plod along we have one speed and that's it.

If you didn't have the feeling you get afterwards, you wouldn't run. It's the satisfaction and the joy of the adrenaline in the body. Your body feels alive. It is talking to you.

3

RUNNING AND PARENTHOOD

For two more weeks, I took it very easy with my ankle injury but absolutely hated having to do so. I did more cross-training at the gym between the ski machine, the bikes and rowing machines. But all the time I was distracted by people on the treadmills, who could run as much or as little as they pleased. I was envious watching them and had to look the other way.

It was killing me that I couldn't get up there and work myself to my limits. I was afraid I might never be able to run again; that some mysterious, serious injury had occurred to my ankle that could be irreparable.

No longer able to train for anything in particular, I found my whole life compromised by a new lack of direction. I couldn't practise running with a view to doing a 10k race or even a half-marathon, because I simply couldn't run at all.

I was shocked at how aimless the whole thing made me feel. I couldn't remember what my goals had been before running or what it was that kept me motivated day to day. Since taking up the sport and falling in love with it, setting ongoing running targets had been keeping me going. They gave me a sense of purpose and all the energy I needed to cope with the demands of my work and family life.

Even the kids couldn't remember the old me. Whenever I donned my running kit and headed outdoors, they would call out, 'Are you going for a run, Mammy?' as if it was the most natural thing in the world. I loved the way the children had adapted so easily to this new passion in my life. To them, running was completely normal and something they did all the time anyway. Sometimes they ran laps around the house with me when we were home together. They talked about running and what a great exercise it was. It was so funny to hear such little people echoing thoughts I had obviously been saying out loud.

Running had also brought extra satisfaction to my social life as I had got into the habit of fitting in training sessions prior to nights on the town, finding that the buzz that came with them only added to my enjoyment of being out and about. Padraic and I often went for workouts together before hitting the pubs on our rare nights out.

As it happened, it took another two weeks to clear my injury completely, which isn't really a long time in terms of the bigger picture – although while I was going through it, it seemed to take forever. I was overjoyed to discover the pain easing off gradually as a result of resting, until at last I could run on the ankle again.

Once more I felt renewed and rejuvenated. Promising myself not to go at things too hard, too soon, I started with a 30-minute trek around one of my favourite circuits. Being out in the open air again, pushing myself and keeping going and going, was the sweetest feeling. I took a break the next day and then the following day, I did a 40-minute session on the treadmill. After that, I worked myself up to three runs a week, all the time taking care to watch the road surfaces, mind my ankle, do my stretches and generally not overdo things.

My high lasted at least another fortnight until another problem arose out of the blue. It was April, the weather had turned cold and conditions weren't too attractive for outdoor pursuits. I persevered with a couple of runs but was finding it difficult to make the time to get out regularly. My family life with four young children was very busy and having to synchronise things with Padraic to fit running space into every second day was proving problematic. I had already given up full-time work to spend more time with the children, so, much as I loved running, I certainly couldn't allow my new pastime to elbow into the space dedicated to my stay-at-home-parenting.

The whole thing started to become an issue. I couldn't give running the attention I wanted to. I also wanted to improve my nutrition, cook healthy meals and eat well, but there wasn't the time to invest in all that while looking after the children. I had to cook simple children's meals and this meant I often had to make do with much the same for myself.

Surprised as I had been to fall in love with running, I was amazed that I seemed to be falling out of love with it as easily. Trying to make time for it added such an amount of extra pressure to my life that it was almost a hassle. I dearly wanted to run but began to wonder was it worth the trouble.

What worried me most of all was that running itself seemed to be becoming a chore. I stopped enjoying it. I continued fitting it in every two or three days, loving how good it made me feel afterwards, but before my runs, I often disliked the very thought of doing them. The passion was fading.

Grainne Cunningham

I do see running as more important now since having the kids. Apart from my first marathon, all I did was prepare for mini-marathons and then let it go. Weeks could go by without me going for a run at all.

Then when I had the kids I used to run as a way to get out for 30 or

40 minutes. It's so intense having triplets. When they're small you would literally be dying to escape as it's a constant slog. The great thing with running was you didn't have to arrange to meet anybody or be anywhere. You could go straight out the door.

The triplets were born in December 2004 and in September 2005 I ran the half-marathon in the Phoenix Park. I wanted to be under two hours.

We had a very hard time the first year with the boys and I remember feeling desperate to the point of wanting to scream. It was hard to survive it without going absolutely nuts. I would feel a sense of panic being left alone with the babies. I would say to Simon, 'You can't leave me alone here.' I remember one day looking out the front door to see if any of my neighbours were in. I was a first-time mother. I was new to it. I didn't know what I was doing and there were three little babies to mind. Simon used to say, ' Go for a run,' because he knew I would come back lighter and easier.

Sometimes I don't know why I feel boxed in or grumpy and then I go for a run and after I do, I'm better. It's much nicer for me now as the boys are older and we're all more relaxed. It's brilliant seeing three little people growing up together and having such different personalities.

When you become a mum-of-triplets your whole identity shifts. You suddenly become the mum-of-triplets all the time. People introduce you and say, 'This is Grainne and she has triplets.' I don't like that. It used to be about who you were.

With running, though, it's just you. In any other area of life there is always another relationship to think about. But it's just you, as you are, not in your role as the mother, the wife, the journalist or anything else, but you, as you were born and will die. You wouldn't get that feeling on a tennis court.

Ray D'Arcy

After Kate was born I bought a baby-jogger, a three-wheeled thing you can run along with. I've only had it out three times now and admit I am a little bit embarrassed about it. Yes, it looks odd. I can see people pointing at it. It does look hilarious. It has inflatable wheels, like a small bike, 20 inches in diameter, which are unbelievably smooth to run with. You're not leaning on it and you know for sure you're running. I'd say you probably use up even more energy than by running alone. The scientific definition of work is to move a weight through a distance, which in effect is what you're doing with a baby-jogger.

Three women did the BUPA run with them. I think what's happening now is that because people are having children later, they've established their hobbies in their twenties and early thirties and don't want necessarily to stop what they've been doing if they have children. So they bring the kids along.

Gerry Galvin

My wife Mary is very supportive of my running and very interested to see how I get on in events. She has come to half-marathons and more but it's not the best spectator sport because you're only going to see the person passing once. But for anything local like the Louisburgh to Westport half-marathon, Mary would be there with the kids and it's nice to have them there. It's so important to have someone at the end, whether it's family or friends or relatives. To have someone there to pick up the pieces is what you need and it can be very emotional when you come over the line. You put so much effort into it that your concentration isn't the best.

Mary and I have four in the family, four kids from six to zero. Before, I used to run during the day but after the kids it never worked out. You have to schedule running around your family life. Night runs work for us because you're with the family during the day when they need you.

It may sound like it's all very self-centred and about me, me, me. But you have to customise your running to suit the family. Running is one thing but you make it suit the kids, your work. You're not going out and saying you won't be back and there's war and there's trouble and the kids are crying when you leave the house. You leave when everyone's happy. When you're going out on a training run, it has to be with one thing in mind and that's the run. You can't be thinking about home, work, money, getting money in, cheques, incidents, computers crashing or anything like that. Make sure there's a happy atmosphere before and after. That's one of the most rewarding things that comes with this package of running and running training. When you're happy in the home, you're happy out running. That's all you want.

4

Injury and Recovery

By this time, I was an avid reader of all things to do with running and had finished reading Paula Radcliffe's autobiography. Her descriptions of marathon training regimes and injury experiences left me marvelling at athletes and the work and preparation they put into excelling at their chosen sport.

I was still confused about what place running had in my own life, and instead of focusing on how well I had been doing, I went through a further period of questioning the whole point of my new running pastime. Where did I really expect running to take me? Was I being unrealistic telling myself I might run a marathon some day – even a half-marathon? Was there really a point to it all?

My longest runs to date had covered five miles and taken me 50 minutes to complete. The last one of these had left me exhausted and disappointed, as I found it such a struggle. I acknowledged that my inner voice had changed from positive to negative. There were other disappointments in my life around this time and looking back, I think these had an effect on my attitude to running.

At any rate I decided to battle on. Whether or not running was for me, I committed myself to keeping at it, vowing to run regularly in the hope that the joy of the sport would return to me once again. If I could retrieve that feeling, I could start planning and aiming for goals once more.

Fortunately, my strategy to run every second day, regardless, stood me in good stead. After persevering for one week, I was back to enjoying running again. The weather had improved too and the outdoors beckoned.

By then, I was in the habit of keeping a training diary and noticed a pattern developing whereby running seemed harder some weeks than others. My age and the fact that hormonal changes were taking place in my body every month didn't escape my notice. I was open to accepting all this as par for the course and getting on with it. It wouldn't last forever.

There was also the advantage that once I had pulled through whatever trying weeks came along, I could look forward to enjoying running all over again. I had learned by then that this would be a pattern in relation to running. There would always be times when it would feel great; there would be other times when it would feel like hell.

The very movements of my arms and legs, the feeling of the wind on my face, nature all around me as I ran – my appreciation for all these things returned. I was glad to be physically capable of running and made a promise to myself that as long as I could run, I would continue to do so.

The blues over with, everything improved. With my running highs back again, I was able to challenge myself further and upped my regular run from three to four miles and on occasion, five. It had taken me some time to reach the five-mile mark and because it was still taking me up to an hour to complete this distance, I needed to concentrate on improving my speeds. I had no reason to believe I wasn't capable of rising to new challenges and was feeling fitter than I had for years and years. I was still carrying at least a stone of extra weight but felt much leaner and more toned.

My mindset had fortunately changed to positive once more. I was buzzing from running and my biggest difficulty was fitting it into my life. If I had had my way, I would have got up early every morning and taken to the highways and byways, but that wasn't possible with family life.

At weekends, though, I relished being able to go for a run while my husband and kids slept. There was never a question of missing a workout. Those two days were sacred to me and I added extra motivation by promising myself breakfast in town afterwards – usually scrambled eggs, toast and lashings of coffee. Just the job.

It was on one of my Saturday morning runs that I finally succeeded in adding a full mile to my five-mile routine. I had read about athletes pushing themselves harder all the time, I knew I could – and had to do it. The fact that I had been a competitive athlete in my early days proved a real driving force.

I still did not have clarity about my ultimate running goal, as by then I had decided a marathon would be too much for me within the space of my first year. My rate of progress was too slow, and running for an hour was tough enough, never mind contemplating keeping going, through thirst, dehydration, toilet needs and other common physical ailments over the course of four hours or more. I was happy to aim for a half-marathon, which I had been advised I should complete at around the two-hour mark. I put my name forward for an event in July, three months away, the first ever Achill half-marathon, believing I could push myself for such a special occasion.

Back to my training: on the day the extra mile didn't prove difficult at all. I was in top form and probably could even have tested myself on a seven-mile run. But with me, it was always a case of being afraid to push myself too hard, too soon. I knew what it felt like to be injured and unable to run at all. I didn't want to jeopardise my performance in any way and I was naturally cautious. I also acknowledged how the six-miler had tested my body. My calf muscles were that bit tighter, my feet actually hurt and I was stiff all over.

The next day I watched the London Marathon TV coverage from start to finish and was riveted by the whole thing. I scrutinised the runners' faces and imagined what was going on in their heads that enabled them to put one foot in front of the other again and again. Seeing so many thousands of people running together all at once gave me a sense of what it must be like to be in a marathon, being pulled along by the flow and encouraged to keep going by all the onlookers.

The TV coverage left me fired up, seeing all those people achieve such a wonderful feat through running – a sport I now accepted I loved more than ever. I wanted to get out there and do the exact same thing. For the first time, I thought that maybe I too had the ability to do what those runners had done. I simply needed to keep on training – train harder and more consistently than ever. Perhaps by the year end, I could have more than a half-marathon under my belt. I might even go for a full marathon too!

This psychological boost took me out of my previous comfort zone of aiming low and playing safe, and threw me into a much more ambitious and driven programme.

Two days later I set out to run seven miles, one more than I had ever managed before, and completed the task. I felt on a roll. I enjoyed the run, my legs felt good, I wanted to challenge myself and after easily coming through my second wind after about 25 minutes of running, I really got into my stride. I delighted in listening to my body as my legs rhythmically moved and hit the ground.

The buzz was fantastic. I was totally in my element. Passing cars, undulating surfaces, racing motorbikes – nothing could take away from the feeling. I was high on life. I was doing something I loved, exerting myself physically, feeling great and up for pushing myself that bit harder with every new step. I experimented with my stride, lengthening it first and then shortening it again, finding I preferred to run more quickly to cover more ground. As I contemplated the end of my usual four-mile course and the start of the three-mile add-on section for the longer run, I had no hesitation about going further. After seeing people completing the marathon, I felt I could easily work to keep going for seven.

Afterwards, I drove back over the route of my run and confirmed that I had covered seven miles. The satisfaction was enormous. I was thrilled with myself – not least because I felt so good physically. Sure, my legs were tired but I no longer seemed to be getting injuries. My ankles felt strong, the soles of my feet were nice and soft and I routinely completed and enjoyed my stretches following every outing. Speaking of stretches, I also decided I was much more elastic than I had given myself credit for; that I could be more flexible and broaden the horizons in my life in general. I decided I would run a marathon before the year was out after all.

In order to take my new challenge seriously, I carried out a review of my training programme to date and discovered I had been running three times a week for most of January, February and March and had increased to four times a week since April.

I immediately committed to a four-times-a-week schedule at the very minimum and, in accordance with various marathon training schedules I had read to date, resolved to increase the intensity and distances of my runs on a gradual basis. I had recorded a total of 18 miles over the previous week – my highest to date – and promised to cover that again, possibly more, over the following week. I remained aware of training advice that recommends you increase your time or length of running by no more than 10% per week.

I began my new regime two days later with an early-morning workout on the treadmill at the gym. I had discovered I was a good early-morning performer and enjoyed waking up with exercise. I intended covering perhaps three to four miles in the gym twice a week, saving my long runs for the weekend and keeping Mondays free to recover.

But once on the treadmill, and after chatting with one of the staff about all the goings-on at the London marathon, I got worked up mentally again and felt like pushing myself. I decided to focus on speed training for a change. So after running at my usual 8kph and prodding it up to a steady paced 10kph, I then did interval training, increasing to 12kph for two to three minutes at a time. I was running all out during what were sprint paces for me and liked having introduced something new to my training again. Because it was new, it felt different and I felt different too. After 40 minutes I decided I'd pushed myself enough. I'd covered almost five miles and could feel in my legs that I'd given myself a right workout.

After doing some stretches, I lay down on a mat to let my body recover. I was amazed at how much the speed training had tested me physically. The heat coming off my chest, around my heart and my tummy, was intense. I was red hot from exertion. I hadn't felt so revved up for ages.

It took a good few minutes for me to cool down again. I usually did a bit of weight training after treadmill sessions but this time decided I done quite enough. I didn't need to prove anything more.

I made one of my biggest mistakes the day after my speed training by prematurely deciding I was recovered from the hard run and capable of hitting the road again. I thought I was refreshed and rearing to go, but it was all in my mind. The problem was that I was so highly psyched up with a view to running a marathon that I was talking myself into excessive training.

People were regularly telling me I was 'looking fit', which was exactly the kind of thing I wanted to hear. I loved going out running and saluting other like-minded runners along the way. I remained deeply motivated and wanted to make more and more progress.

Unfortunately, I was forgetting how very important it was to let your muscles recover after a heavy bout of exercise. I had been good at taking my rest days up to this but because I was making such progress, I somehow convinced myself I didn't need so much rest any more. Wasn't I fit enough not to need to rest!

This approach became my downfall and resulted in my losing almost another month of proper training. I did a second hard run on the road the day after my speed training on the treadmill, covering seven miles, and for the last stretch, I actually had to run with a limp.

My old left ankle injury resurfaced slightly, but an altogether new tenderness developed in the ball of my foot. It wasn't a specific injury and again I knew it required rest to heal. But I didn't want to rest. I took it easy for a day or two but by day three, I longed to push myself flat out again.

In any event, I couldn't. Not physically. My injury was referring from my left toe to the ball of my foot to my ankle and even up to my knee and hip. Every bit of exercise I did seemed to make things worse. I was left with no option but to rest completely.

Fear played a big part in my reluctance to stop running again as I had read about athletes who lost their fitness completely after two to three weeks' rest. My biggest concern as always was that if I did give up running, I would never run again. The sheer effort of having overcome my dislike of running in the first place, and the extra effort I had invested in improving my running times and distances, had required a huge level of dedication and commitment. I was afraid that if I gave myself a break from that self-imposed pressure (which I enjoyed in a sort of a love/hate way at times), I would be mentally unable to go back and start all over again.

At any rate I was forced to cut back my running to allow my foot to heal. Mentally, I changed from being totally driven to run and build up my mileage, to suffering anew from self-doubt. Perhaps I wasn't cut out to be a runner after all. Maybe 40 was too old to take up an exercise as demanding as running.

For the next three weeks, I remained unsure of myself. I started taking less care of my diet and generally grew more and more frustrated. While one part of my inner self was telling me to throw the towel in on this 'whole running lark', a bigger part was yelling at me not to dare give up. I had to persevere because it was in my nature to be highly competitive. If I gave up, it would mean failure.

It's amazing how the power of the mind is revealed as the strongest factor at such times. I was aware that my situation was totally a case of mind over matter. I had talked myself into becoming obsessive about running. I could as easily talk myself into keeping going, even if I wasn't physically able to do so for a spell.

In the end, I again made the decision that I would keep going, at whatever level I could. I would plough on and not even entertain the thought of giving up; and I would review my situation a week at a time.

Over the three weeks of recuperation, I continued reading up on athletes' life stories, marathons and anything to do with physical training. I had never been interested in mountain climbing but read Joe Simpson's excellent works on the subject and was fired up by them too. Anything to do with athletic conditioning, overcoming obstacles and pushing the human spirit in order to achieve a physical challenge, became a must-read for me. Jane Tomlinson, a British woman who worked through terminal cancer to run marathons and then triathlons and who has since died at the age of 43, provided further inspirational fuel in her touching autobiographical works. I felt it was important to use other people's stories to keep myself going and to motivate myself to continue with my dream to train for and run a marathon.

Gradually, by the middle of May, my foot started feeling less tender. I invested in another new pair of running shoes and found they helped my recovery.

As the weeks passed and I continued running to whatever extent I was capable of, I came to accept certain things about my chosen sport. Firstly, I was confident that running was the right exercise for me at the time, as, with a bit of work, I could fit it around my busy schedule and didn't have to depend on anyone else to get going. I truly loved everything it entailed – the full use of body and limbs, the total exertion it demanded, and especially the fact that all I needed was a good pair of runners to get started.

Secondly, I realised that my love for the sport wouldn't inspire me every time I needed to go for a run. Regularly, it would be a case of mind over matter. I often didn't feel like going running. It was the knowledge of all the good it was doing me and the great buzz it guaranteed me afterwards that actually got me to the point of putting on my trainers.

Thirdly, I knew I had to give myself goals in order to keep at it. Doing that was important because Mother Nature seemed to have programmed a pretty strong negative inner voice in me during times of weakness or doubt.

While my ultimate goal was always to run a marathon, I had

also registered that the training involved should set me up as a regular runner for the rest of my active days and that was the real goal I wanted to achieve.

I was delighted, by early June, to have notched my training back up to around 20 miles per week. The first ever Achill half-marathon I had entered was due to take place on 1 July and gave me exactly the focus I needed. I had been half-planning to run my first half-marathon at a local event later on, in mid-August, but felt that having so much time to train to cover 13 miles had been making me quite sloppy about my schedule. Sometimes I ran five miles, sometimes seven and sometimes I felt like cutting off after three.

So by bringing the deadline forward for the 13-mile mark, I really had no choice but to apply myself immediately to building up my distances. That obligation changed my perspective instantly. I geared myself up for my longest run ever, opting to do it on the treadmill at the gym as I had been having regular injury problems from my runs outdoors. My longest outdoor run by the end of May was over 10k, about seven miles, which I did one glorious evening when the roads were quiet and I felt I could run forever. Since then, I had never done less than a 5k run at a time and was looking forward to exceeding my 10k performance. Now was my chance.

I covered 10k on the treadmill in under an hour, satisfied I was keeping to 5k in 30 minutes. I felt good and was motivated even further by the fact that Paul, the gym supervisor, was monitoring my effort and knew I wanted to push myself further.

I got to 12k, still feeling good, and decided I would go for 15k in total. By 14k, I was struggling like never before. My stomach was acting up. I got a stitch in my side, my breathing became strained and real fatigue started setting in. At more than 90 minutes, I completed 15k. However, the fixed programme on the treadmill told me I had nine more minutes to go. I had always been tantalised by this programme and because I was so close now to the end, I decided to keep going.

I lowered my speed from 10k to 8k and, pretty much in pain by then, kept jogging. I was aware that the big toe on my right foot was hurting every time I ran on it. I had already lost the nail on my left foot, which was still growing back. I didn't really want to have to go through that experience all over again.

Finally, as I hit 16k, the programme ended with the customary 'Great Workout' salute, which I particularly relished on that occasion. I cooled down and assessed my performance. I was knackered but elated. I had never felt such fatigue in my legs or muscles. I saw it as a priority to do a good stretching session afterwards, which I'm sure stood to me over the next few days. My recovery was quick enough, in that I was able to walk at least! But boy, did I experience real muscle fatigue. I used up 1100 calories in the workout and my body demanded frequent carbohydrate-rich meals to recuperate.

Sure enough, after my 16k run, my right toenail came off. I took two complete days off afterwards from running. On the third day I still didn't really feel like getting going again but by then, was only too familiar with that mindset. I simply had to talk myself through it. I didn't ever want to let three days go between training runs. I knew how easily that could become four days, then five and so on.

Even though I had repeatedly told myself by then that I was a runner, my deep fear remained that some day soon it would all stop; that I would give up on my dream. I still had a long way to go to build up my own self-confidence.

5

TRAINING FOR MY FIRST HALF-MARATHON

Almost as if I had willed it to happen, my dream of running in the 2006 Achill half-marathon dissolved after I was struck down with an extremely debilitating summer virus. One moment I was planning my running schedule for the week and the next, I could barely walk. My entire body seized up with aches and pains that lasted for two solid weeks, rendering me dizzy and weak for a third week and just about in recovery mode by week four. So driven was I to fulfil my half-marathon ambition that while in the first stages of the illness, I stupidly forced myself on to the treadmill at the gym. After one minute of running, my chest and lungs throbbed with pain. It felt like the coldest frost-laden air of winter had filled my throat. I had to stop.

Two days later, when I was still no better but convincing myself otherwise, the treadmill beckoned again. This time I forced myself to run through the pain, telling myself it would go away if I ran through it. It didn't. Having pushed as far as 3k, my body could go no further. I showered, changed and returned home, dejected and disgusted. I knew I had done even more damage in my denial of the illness. Not only would I have to cancel my date with the July half-marathon, I might not even be ready for the August event.

The disappointment was overwhelming. I could barely tolerate the illness, let alone deal with the destruction of my dream. The only way I managed to get through that time was by making myself look at the bigger picture. My dream was a mere drop in the ocean compared to all the worthwhile things that needed to be achieved in my life. I looked at the news and reminded myself how good I had it compared to so many others.

This worked a bit, but not completely. However pathetic my dreams, they were still my dreams and, consequently, very important to me. All the books I had read about other people pursuing their sporting ambitions told me that the targets they set for themselves were all that mattered to them too. It seemed to me that many people made sense of their lives by setting specific goals, sporting or otherwise. My sporting goal fitted in well with the other aspects of my life and involved doing something I loved and that kept me motivated, energetic and filled with a sense of purpose. I could not bear to give it up.

I stuck it out because I had to of course, taking my antibiotics and multivitamins as prescribed. But I didn't do it with a heart and a half. Ultimately, my so-called summer virus turned into something much more ominous when, after six weeks solid of feeling horribly unwell, I was diagnosed with an overactive thyroid.

I learned that the thyroid gland, located in the neck, controls the body's metabolism with its production of the hormone thyroxine. If the flow of thyroxine is interfered with, the levels of hormone secreted can rise or fall. In my case, thyroxine levels rose, the consequences of which included a speeded-up metabolism and a rapid and strong heartbeat that hammered so hard in my chest I expected to have a heart attack any minute. Obviously, running was out of the question.

During the period of my illness, the two half-marathons that I so badly wanted to participate in came and went. My husband Padraic, who had also been running regularly, mostly on the treadmill, actually took my place in the first ever Achill half-marathon, and had no trouble at all completing the course in a good time around the 2 hr 30 mark. He looked fantastic at the finish line, like a young man all over again, and I could see looking at him how running benefits a person in mind, body and soul. It was great to celebrate his achievement, although of course there was a bittersweet element in it for me. But being there on the day and watching all the participants did my heart good. Achill is such a beautiful part of the world and the organisers of the event were very helpful, letting Padraic take my place and handing out complimentary t-shirts to all our kids.

While I deeply regretted missing out on the event, my illness was affecting me so badly that the very thought of exercise seemed to hurt. My symptoms included aching muscles and joints, feelings of burning up, sweating, weakness and dizziness, pains in my heart after the slightest exertion (housework included!), feeling tired all the time, being hyperactive all day before collapsing in the evening, disturbed sleep and breathlessness. By the time of my diagnosis, I was a full stone lighter.

When my condition was definitively diagnosed the following week, I was prescribed the thyroid drug I needed. After one day of taking the medication I felt completely different. I knew my sickness had been hit spot-on for the first time. The correct dosage had yet to be ascertained, but I was on the road to recovery at last.

When you are sick, your mind becomes absorbed with the sickness, thinking about it and the symptoms, figuring out how it will be treated and hoping to get better. Things that were a priority quickly get shunted down the line.

That was how it came to be with my running ambitions. Of course one part of me wished I were still training, feeling on top form and working towards my half-marathon and marathon goals. But the bigger part of me, the part concerned with my basic need to survive, was totally focused on getting better.

So it was that I was able to put running out of my thoughts all the time I was sick and recovering. The fact that I began to feel a bit normal again after taking the thyroid drug comforted me with the possibility that I might recover fully, that I might be myself once more. Living with that hope was all that mattered. I longed to have my health back.

After a few weeks on medication I knew I wasn't anywhere near as sick as when my condition had gone untreated. My passion for running hadn't gone away entirely and as my spirits lifted overall, I decided to take advantage of my good days by doing whatever bit of running felt right. I started by running one kilometre and then kept it between three and five kilometres, in the gym only. I had decided to cut out outdoor runs completely until I felt fully better and enjoyed being back in the Beech Club, soaking up the communal 'working out' environment and availing of the excellent equipment and pool and leisure centre there.

I was grateful to be able to run at all again. My illness had cast doubts over my health in general. To learn from my doctor that I should recover completely was such a blessing. By all accounts, thyroid conditions are among the easiest illnesses to treat.

As time went on, a new sense of confidence returned, as the highs and lows in my condition became less pronounced, and I made the decision to set myself some goals again. I was never unrealistic about what I hoped to do. My aim had been to run a half-marathon, with any notion of running a full marathon to be determined by the outcome of that goal. However, in the light of my circumstances, I needed to revise my running goals and set myself an easier challenge to start off with again. As Christmas was around the corner again, I decided I would be very happy to complete the annual St Stephen's Day 5k fun run again.

A few days before the event, I was back on one of my regular four-mile outdoor runs when the big toe on my right foot suddenly started to throb. It turned out that the new running shoes I had been breaking in were too tight at the top and when I ran downhill, the pressure was too great. By the time I showered and changed, I could see the tenderness wouldn't be a temporary thing. My toenail was clearly turning black and all around the skin was red, tender and sore-looking. Over the next day or two my toe got worse, instead of better, and the injury seemed to be festering all around the sides. I knew I couldn't train again before the fun run and instead set about enjoying the family Christmas as much as possible. I wasn't backing out of the event, though, and when the big day arrived, I planned to go and do my thing all over again.

The weather on that morning was absolutely beautiful, bone-dry, nice and fresh but not too cold. It was great to find myself in amongst a bunch of runners again, even if a whole year had passed since my first such outing. The fact that it was the same 5k event and not a bigger challenge wasn't important. Despite being another year older, at least I wasn't going downhill.

Unfortunately, even with my happy state of mind, buoyed up once more by the support of Padraic and the kids egging me on, physically I wasn't feeling up to scratch on the day and struggled throughout the entire course. My sore toe certainly put me out a bit but there was more to it than that. I felt out of sorts and knew it was all down to my thyroid. I couldn't hurry its recovery. Worse still, at the half-way mark I developed an agonising stitch that would not go away, even though I held my abdomen with one hand all the way back to the finish line.

Ernie Caffrey,
beside his 25mph treadmill

Grainne Cunningham,
marathon runner

*Mary Walsh, three-time
New York marathoner*

*Mary Kennedy, RTÉ, twice .
the Dublin marathon (© RT*

*Professor Risteárd Mulcah.
ran his first marathon at si.*

*Ray D'Arcy,
Today FM keep-fit fan
(© Today FM)*

Gerry Galvin, marathon runner

*Dr Mick Loftus,
community activist and runner*

Padraic Geraghty after the Achill half-marathon, July 2006

Joan waits it out with Mary (left) and Helen at the Achill half-marathon

The Geraghty boys, Peter and Nathan, take turns with Dad's half-marathon medal

Joan's training buddies, Noreen O'Toole and Jason O'Brien

The start of the Connemara half-marathon, 1 April 2007

Joan heading off on the Connemara half-marathon

Over at last! Joan with her Connemara half-marathon medal

With Joan Rowland before the Achill half-marathon, 2007

Joan and Padraic after finishing the Achill half-marathon, 2007

In the end, I did succeed in beating my performance time of 12 months before and was genuinely surprised to learn that I came in at 29 minutes 11 seconds – below the half-hour mark. For me, it was a personal best. On the treadmill I had once managed to complete 5k in a bit more than 27 minutes but running indoors is much easier.

My running took off badly in the New Year when, after two more weeks of training on my sore toe, I had to give up again because of the pain. Finally, I took myself off to the doctor who took one look at it and declared it badly infected and requiring immediate treatment. I was told a course of antibiotics would right everything and that without these, the infection could work itself up my leg.

The whole thing got me thinking about how keeping good form is one of the most difficult and precarious balancing acts for a sportsperson, at any level. The body may often be likened to a machine but its individual functions are so variable and separate that nobody can predict how they will perform on a given day.

The power of the mind is another massive factor in relation to performance. Even being in top physical condition cannot guarantee what will happen. The slightest thing from a verbal putdown to the feeling of a stitch coming on can knock you sideways.

Fortunately for me, my running form improved as January 2007 moved on and my toe infection cleared completely. My thyroid condition also seemed to be stabilising at last, and I reduced my medication to the minimum dose of 5mg a day – a maintenance level.

At the end of January, I sent off a completed entry form to run my first half-marathon (again) on 1 April (April Fools!). The event was one of the challenges in the Connemara Marathon 2007 calendar, which included a full marathon and ultra-marathon, and, by all accounts, covered an extremely hilly and demanding course. In the spot where it asked what time you expected to complete the run in, I wrote 'two hours' – which would have been very good for me. Well, I had to remain optimistic.

By the middle of January, my thyroid problem had stabilised well enough for me to finally start building up my fitness again. On the second Sunday in the month, I went out on what had become my regular 10k run and added an extra loop of 4k. I wasn't necessarily feeling in top form but wanted to see could I really stretch myself again at last. Approaching the turn into the extra loop (the hilly Cloona circuit), I assessed how I felt and thought I could do it. I covered the extra ground without too many problems, really enjoying the new challenge, then came back out on to my original route with 4k more to run. That last part was difficult as my legs felt drained from having to keep going for so long. But I persevered, trying to work on my speed too but without actually doing any sprints. I was too exhausted.

Finally I completed the course and discovered I had been running for one hour and 28 minutes – the longest I'd ever kept going for. It wasn't a fast time by most standards but for me, it was good and I was happy with it. I calculated that had I kept going for another 7k, to make up the 21k of a half-marathon, I might have finished in 2 hours 15 minutes. Given that I had estimated my completion time on the Connemara half-marathon at two hours, evidently I still had some training to do. At that stage I was thrilled I had managed to keep running over such a distance and was newly confident I could complete a half-marathon. It might take months of training for me to reach that goal but I was in no hurry and only wanted to prove to myself I could do it.

During February and March I maintained as consistent a running programme as possible with a view to being ready for my first half-marathon. It was great having a specific target date in mind and once I started an actual countdown from eight weeks onwards, time passed very quickly.

The month of February was especially busy as for work reasons I had to travel to Dublin on two successive weekends. I was thrilled at one point to find myself running in Phoenix Park. For the hundreds and thousands of people who run the length and breadth of Phoenix Park on a regular basis, covering the 5km distance from the entrance gates off Conyngham Road through to the exit gates to Castleknock might be no big deal. For me, though, it was a major buzz. It wasn't just the wonderful expanse of green parkland and the myriad walking/running paths throughout that appealed to me. The big attraction was being able to be among so many other people out running and loving it.

It was a Saturday morning when I joined my friend Helen and another pal for their weekly run in the Phoenix Park; by all accounts, Saturdays and Sundays are the busiest days there for runners. We arrived at 10am and already the grounds were lined with people running along every track in sight. I had never before been among such a throng of casual runners and enjoyed a new sense of belonging. I wasn't the lone runner taking to the highways and byways any more. I was one of them. Watching the various running groups, clubs and individuals training alongside each other that day proved fascinating and gave me another tremendous lift.

For most of February I managed to run consistently and that bit harder, faster and longer than before. All the time I was aware that the deadline for my half-marathon event was fast approaching and I really wanted to be as well prepared as possible.

For my long run one Sunday morning, feeling in top physical

form and positive mentally, I decided to keep going as far as my legs would carry me. By this point I had gained a running partner, Noreen, who worked in the gym. She was also intending to run in the Connemara marathon event and was ready to push herself harder. Unfortunately, due to a bad cold, she had to cry off our run on that particular morning.

So I hit the road all by myself again and started off intending to complete the 10k loop I was familiar with. Along the way, though, I unintentionally took a detour (a wrong turn) and in the course of running this new stretch, realised it would add an extra 5k at least to my journey, making it my longest run to date (if I could complete it).

I kept my head down and applied myself to the task. It was a glorious morning, nice and cold, dry and with the faintest of winds. The detour meant I was going along stretches of roads I had never run before and the novelty of that made for a truly enjoyable experience as I relished the natural beauty around me.

I was running well, feeling good, keeping a consistent pace of about 10km an hour and breathing softly and rhythmically. It was all going swimmingly well until I returned to the path I had veered from and estimated that there was about 5km left to run.

From then on I began to suffer. I had been running for approximately an hour already and although I was happy to note that my legs still felt pretty good, the same couldn't be said for my insides. Basically, I was dying to go to the toilet! There were a number of problems though. First of all, I was running along a popular walking trail and while there were other people about, there was no such thing as a public convenience. Secondly, I knew that if I was to succeed in relieving myself, I would have to stop running, something I was not prepared to do. Thirdly, while I could steel myself to run through the pain and sheer discomfort, I would have to slow down to make it to the end. So I did slow down and over the course of the next half hour, I think I had my first experience of 'hitting the wall', although not on a marathon run.

It was so surreal it felt almost like an out-of-body experience. While I kept moving one leg after the other, mentally I was in another realm. Cars and other people out walking passed me by but for me they were in a haze. All my energies were focused on keeping myself going physically. Mentally however, I was pretty much ga ga. It constituted sheer mind over matter-ness as my inner voice commanded me, mantra-like, to keep running. I'm only glad someone didn't stop and try to talk to me while I was in that state, as God knows what they might have heard.

I remained in that mental limbo until the very end of the run and while I was exhilarated to have kept going to the finish, it felt different to my normal post-run high. Even though at 15k, it marked my longest ever run on the road (I had managed 16k on the treadmill), I didn't feel the anticipated thrill from my achievement. The mental strain I endured in order to complete the run left me feeling I had done something wrong, rather than something right, with that particular outing.

Overall, I was filled with a sense of disappointment, which was extremely surprising. The truth was, I felt I had pushed myself too far physically. I felt I'd overdone it and that I had been wrong to put my body through such a trial.

There was a positive aspect though. In the run I had covered almost 16km, which was 5km short of what the half-marathon event would be. Because I was still pretty wired at the 16km stage and only stopped because my goal had been reached, I felt that had the goal been that bit further (5km even), I would have been able to reach that too. In other words, for the first time since my running training began, I really did feel I was physically (whatever about mentally) capable of completing my targeted half-marathon event. So that was a plus.

But my residual feeling was that pushing myself too far took away from the joy of running. My plan from then on was to complete the half-marathon event as planned, then return to running reasonable distances for the fun of it.

Two days later, I was back on the roads again, loving it and pooh-poohing my previous lily-livered attempt to get out of hard training. After one day's recovery from my 10-miler, I felt renewed and refreshed and belatedly elated at having managed the distance. I was feeling good and wanted to keep pushing myself further. In actual fact, I was on a course to enjoying possibly my highest ever level of wellbeing.

The final month of my training turned out to be an amazing experience in every way. At the last minute, I decided I would commit to using my run to fund-raise, and picked no less a cause than play facilities at our children's national school.

Padraic, my husband, printed out a load of sponsorship forms for me and so I had no choice but to approach people I knew with my half-marathon plans. My running was out in the open for everyone to know about. My name was on the form with the date of the scheduled event.

Immediately, I felt under a completely new kind of pressure. Running for yourself is one thing but running for a cause is a different kettle of fish. I knew I was up to tapping people for sponsorship because I liked doing that kind of thing, but getting money subject to me performing a real-live run over a distance of 13 miles felt scary. The fact that nobody had ever known me as a runner before also worried me, but need not have. The response I got from people was positive from the off. Most people I asked to sponsor me directly or to take a sponsorship form on my behalf were hugely supportive and I was pleasantly surprised by people's generosity.

'Fair play to you,' I was told over and over again.

Naturally, I persevered in my training with new drive and energy after that. With one month to go, I resolved to train as hard as I could. Following my day of rest after the 10-mile road run, I ran my usual 10k loop, but with another new personal best of 52 minutes – two full minutes quicker than my previous PB. (Knowing that real athletes can complete 10k in in under 30 minutes always helped keep my progress in perspective but in terms of my own ability, evidently, the training was paying off.)

I decided I owed it to myself to keep pushing even harder over the course of the next few weeks as my big event drew nearer.

The following Sunday Noreen and I covered 8.4 miles by adding on a new detour to the 10k loop. Noreen (who loves doing the maths) calculated afterwards that we had covered the distance at an average ten minutes per mile, which we were both happy enough with. We knew we hadn't killed ourselves in the process and had actually held back some. We felt we could do better, which added even further fuel to our training.

The following Friday, Noreen introduced me to her triathlon-loving cousin, Jason, who had offered to do some speed training with us. Suddenly, instead of going it alone on roadsides at whatever pace suited me, I was doing most of my training with people equally interested, if not more interested, in fitness and challenging themselves.

It was fantastic having teamed up with a running buddy at this stage and even better for me, because Noreen was a good bit ahead in fitness and speed and also more than ten years younger. Originally a soccer player, she had been running for years following training with Westport Athletic Club and had learned to lengthen her stride and run fast uphill. Being pushed harder again by Jason, a veteran endurance performer, was even more beneficial to me, although, of course, I didn't think so at the time.

On our first workout together as a threesome, Jason led us to the local track at Westport Sports Complex and over the course of a half-hour, had us speed up and slow down over successive laps. Given that speed training was a completely new concept for me as I had mostly run at whatever pace suited me up until then, I found this experience extremely trying. I started getting flashbacks to when I was around 12 years of age and availed of a brief membership of Castlebar Athletic Club. I recalled the excellent coach there at the time, Vincent McDermott, urging us kids to run faster and faster and the sick feeling in my poor legs as I longed to give up, unlike the many young athletes alongside me who simply excelled at the sport. As far as I remember, I did give up shortly after that. I decided back then I wasn't made to run. But look at me now!

The day after the speed training I could feel my thigh muscles aching and it was sore to stretch or move too much. It was obvious that the sprinting had challenged my body in a different way and I liked the feeling of having done something new. I acknowledged that I had been chugging along for a while again doing my own bits and pieces of running as I chose, but with a few weeks to go to the half-marathon, it felt like a good time to try and up the pace a little.

Two days later, Noreen and I hooked up again for a long run but because of the gale force wind and biting cold rain, we opted instead to cover the 10k loop as fast as we could. With her long stride, Noreen was able to cover the mileage faster than me but she kindly stayed a little in front, pacing me most of the way. At about the half-way mark, the sick feeling that occurred during the speed session returned. I knew I was pushing myself pretty much as hard as I could but because we had abandoned doing a long run, I committed to keeping up the pace the whole way around. It was a struggle. A real struggle. Mentally I talked myself through it, as ever, and having Noreen in front of me was a great bonus. On the last leg downhill to the gym, which we usually sprinted over anyway, I found myself running so fast that I was almost out of control. My legs were frozen and wet through from the rain, I was feeling sick all over from the massive exertion and knew I was mili-seconds from turning head over heels and finishing off the run in a series of tumble-the-wildcats. Happily it didn't come to that. I arrived shortly after Noreen and she clocked our time at 49 minutes 30 seconds – two and a half minutes quicker than my previous record. Another personal best.

With three weeks to go before the big run, Noreen, Jason and I trained together pretty much as a team, pushing ourselves as much as possible. We met two or three times during the week and saved our endurance training for the long Sunday sessions. Amazingly, after a couple of speed training workouts, I did start running faster, even if making the effort to do so generally exhausted me. The fact that I wasn't running faster for myself either, but that I was simply trying to keep up with my running mates, was additionally demanding.

Noreen and Jason made it clear that they believed in me from the outset and were very supportive, running alongside me during our outings until I got my second wind at least. When they eventually got that bit ahead, it was never so far as to disappear out of sight, which could have made me want to give up altogether. Such subtle encouragement convinced me that I simply had to work as part of a team. It became of paramount importance to me not to let my running mates down.

When I think back on that time, it's fascinating to note how rarely we allowed any negative comments to enter our conversations.

On the third Sunday before D-Day, we completed a fabulous 10-mile run with Noreen arriving back in 90 minutes, Jason in 92 minutes and myself in an unbelievable (for me) 96 minutes. Of course we knew we hadn't broken any course records but that didn't stop us being pleased as punch with ourselves.

I was ecstatic because I had had to push myself very hard simply to keep the two of them in sight. In relation to running, I discovered that I tend to go at it quite sharply from the start but then after around the third mile, I start to flag a bit. If I can't flag as much as I would like to, my body starts doing strange things. Instead of letting me throw one foot in front of the other in my usual straight-ish running line, my limbs seem to fly about all over the place. It feels like my natural running gait and body posture dissolve in the sheer effort to keep pace.

During a day-trip to Galway, I gave myself a break from the pressure and sneaked in a fabulous run alone along the prom. Over the course of an hour I blended in with the many other runners enjoying the feeling of stretching their limbs, and actually took some time out to look at the gorgeous views of Galway Bay. I've often read pieces by runners waxing lyrical about the beauty of the scenery around them as they go along but keeping my eyes on the road in front of me is all I can usually manage. Being able to take my time over my running again did give me the opportunity to enjoy my surroundings and this lovely break from my hard training reminded me all over again why I love running for fun. It's exhilarating.

When I returned the next day for yet another killer session, Jason emphasised the benefits of speed training for marathon running. A few days later we did the 10k loop together again and once more I broke my record by almost a minute, completing it in 48 minutes

18 seconds. Jason was correct. The speed training, bad as it was, certainly paid dividends.

With D-Day approaching, we finally got to the wonderful stage of being able to pare down our training in order to be sufficiently rested for the event – well, supposedly at least. With two 10-mile runs under our belt we decided to do one final long run of 11 miles and after that to reduce the distance.

The Sunday for the 11-miler happened to fall on Mother's Day, the day after St Patrick's Day. Weatherwise, things couldn't have been worse. There were onshore gale-force winds, hail, sleet and snow showers and because it was a holiday weekend, most of the cars in Ireland seemed to have converged on the lovely tourist haven of Westport. Our route ran the full length of the coastal road from Louisburgh to Westport – directly in the path of those awful gales and along one of the busiest roads in the whole country that day.

The one good thing was that the wind was on our backs, which meant that we were pushed along stretches of the road. At times, I was actually hoisted up off the ground and lifted by my full weight from one running stride to the next. I had to work hard even to keep my balance. Eventually, we made it back to the Westport Woods Hotel – our starting point – and calculations quickly showed that we had run 20 kilometres – one kilometre short of a half-marathon. It had taken me two hours and ten minutes to cover the distance. I was exhausted but still standing. Definitely, the Connemara was within my grasp.

6

Running My First Half-Marathon

April Fool's Day 2007 finally came and with its passing, I at last became a half-marathoner. On that glorious day in the village of Leenane, County Galway, I headed through the spectacular scenic pass between the Connemara Mountains and on to the finish 13 miles away at remote Maam Cross, amongst a jostling crowd of 3,000 runners. It was an experience I never want to forget as it marked the culmination of such a long and arduous course of training and discipline in my life. But all my commitment paid off in the end. I was up for the task on the day in hand, even though I did give in at the 11-mile stage and walked up part of the 'Hell of the West'. Once over the crest again however, I continued running, pushing myself hard all the way over the course of the final two miles.

My finishing time didn't create any new record. I crossed the line after 2 hours 25 minutes and I was thrilled to have made it within the 2 hour 30 mark, which had been my outer limit. I learned from the experience of running a half-marathon event with thousands of others that many, many strange things can happen along the way as the voice in your head constantly changes tack. After getting away well and keeping up with the general posse for the first eight miles, at mile nine, out of the blue, I opted to stop in my tracks at the water point to drink (something I had refused ever to allow myself do in my training). This meant I wasn't running or even jogging, after over an hour getting into a stride. The effect of this break was like turning off the ignition in a car. I basically cut out.

Even worse, I availed of one of the mini Mars bars offered along the route, taking time out to eat it and savour each mouthful. I now know that such a major break at this stage proved my downfall and can't even explain why I let myself stop in the first place. I had always said I would never stop during a run because I reckoned I might never start again. The problem was that the temptation proved too much. It was such a perfect day with the sun shining like gold above us. I had a cap with a visor on to reduce some of the impact of the sun's rays but still, it felt too nice to be running. All I could see ahead of me was uphill and I was aware that the coming two miles would prove extremely trying. In a sense, I think I temporarily gave up once I stopped. I felt myself going off track; questioning why was I putting myself through such a difficult time on such a fabulous day; why did I need to run 13 miles exactly – hadn't I done well enough to run nine?

The only way I can explain my lack of focus at that stage was in connection with the week's events leading up to the half-marathon. I suffered a severe case of gastrorenteritis, due, I believe, to drinking contaminated water in Galway. For four days I could barely move or eat. I lost a half-stone in weight and barely managed to mind the kids and the house through this time. I invested so much of my energies into getting myself well enough to turn up for my big day that I lost sight of the actual half-marathon itself and what it was all about. I didn't think the course through or formulate a plan of action for how to cope with it, and, more importantly, didn't commit myself to not stopping throughout the race. All I thought about was being well enough to run on the day.

I started running, aimlessly really. It was two weeks since our 20k training run. As Noreen reminded me at the start, I had put the training in. I was up to the 13 miles. Unfortunately though, I was more psyched up for that training run than the event itself. The gap in training due to my sickness left me disorientated and I lost my direction. Everything was so new: the route, being surrounded by thousands of other runners, the water stops, the mile markers, the walkers along the way – it all felt surreal.

That is the only way I can explain why I allowed myself to stop and why, two miles later, I gave in along with so many others to the temptation to walk up the hill which never seemed to end. I started well and finished well, but somewhere in the middle, things went wrong. After that, running felt much harder. I'd had a taste of what it would be like to stop and was lured into a stop-start frame of mind. I basically had to struggle against stopping again all the way to the finish and for the first time ever in my running experience, started wheezing so badly I could barely breathe. I counteracted this by inhaling only through my nose, expelling the air quickly again, but found this an added stress.

Pushing myself so hard over the last two miles left me feeling dangerously exhausted. I arrived at the finish, needing water but unable to get any due to the cattle-mart effect of too many runners crowding together into a seriously small marquee. I left the tent, going outside again for air. I leaned against a car and immediately felt terrible. The wheezing started again, I grew dizzy and developed a sudden and severe headache. Fortunately Noreen came to my rescue then and got me the water I needed as well as an energy drink. I didn't want to talk or do anything that might weaken me further. I stayed like that for about five minutes, gradually feeling my strength return.

At the beginning of the race I had also told Noreen I planned to run my own run. I was trying to avoid any pressure and wanted Noreen to run the best she could, without having to worry about me. Her aim was to keep up with Jason and happily, she performed fabulously on the day, arriving at the finish seconds after the two-hour mark. A fantastic performance for a first half-marathon. Jason had also been extremely sick with throat trouble the week prior to the event but still put in a fine turn, arriving minutes after Noreen. In hindsight, I think if I had put myself under pressure to run alongside Noreen, it might have helped me, as we were used to running together and I could always depend on her to pull me along. I'm not suggesting I could have kept up with her all the way, but I might not have stopped.

At any rate there's no point dwelling any further on the what-ifs or might-have-beens about my own race experience. It's crazy to feel let down after doing a half-marathon when all I ever set out to do was to make it to the finish line. But I've discovered that many, many people feel let down after a race ends. Even in the course of speaking to some of the runners featured in this book whose achievements I admired in completing marathons, multi-marathons and race events, often they dismissed my admiration, usually with the assertion that they should have done better – were it not for one interfering factor or other putting them off their stride.

My own first reaction at finally reaching the finish line at Connemara was that it had all been a pointless experience. I announced to Noreen that that was it. I would never run again, never mind run any long-distance event. I realised the next day though, when the elation at my achievement finally hit me, that it had all been a state of mind; that everything truly is a state of mind. My biggest mistake was that I had forgotten to congratulate myself for achieving the goal I had set out for myself such a long time before. I had trained enormously to meet that goal and had been facing into it with both trepidation and longing as I consistently increased my training. The whole process of readying myself for the task had taken me a year longer than anticipated. But I needed to acknowledge how astonishing it was that I ever made it that far in the first place.

Considering that I had started my running on a treadmill on the basis of two-minute trots followed by five-minute walks, it seemed almost incredible that I should have graduated to half-marathon running. Over the course of my training I had lost over a stone and a half in weight, changed my entire body shape from flabby to lean and boosted my sense of general wellbeing enormously. I had lost sight of all this in my disappointment with my performance on the day. I think the same thing happens any time you set goals and up the ante again and again in order to achieve them. You forget how slow, how inexperienced, how unfit you were at the start. You rate yourself on your most recent performance only, somehow forgetting your original state, but it's so important to take account of where the journey started.

Fortunately, two days after Connemara I was back doing what I truly love, running for fun, health and vitality.

In July 2007 I completed the first Achill half-marathon in 2 hours 7 minutes (almost 20 minutes faster than my first half-marathon performance). And in August 2007 I ran the Louisbourgh–Westport half-marathon in 2 hours 4 minutes. Obviously my first running goal in 2008 is to complete a half-marathon in under two hours. After that a full marathon will beckon again!

7

Runners on Marathon Running

Grainne Cunningham

I did my first marathon in 2002, the year I got married. Even on my honeymoon in August I used to go running. I had done all the small runs, from 5ks to 10-milers and thought, I can go for the marathon. In hindsight, I think you really need to prepare instead of doing it to get around the course.

It was another four years and after we had the triplets before I ran a marathon again. I started back pretty gradually with slow runs at first. I was doing a bit of yoga and met a girl who liked running. We teamed up and she was naturally faster than me and suddenly it was a lot more serious and I decided to go for the half-marathon.

Then it became a sort of lifeline. I went on a speed training session with this guy on a Saturday morning in winter 2005. He said to me, 'What's your goal?' and I said, 'The marathon,' and that was that. It was like it was decided there and then. I did a few more speed-training sessions after that. I learned from them and that's when I decided to join the Bray Runners.

I think sub-four hours is the big one that people aim for. Everybody recognises it is a barrier in marathon running. You see it at the end of marathons, a mass of people coming in at or around the four-hour mark. It's 26 miles so if you can run consistent nine-minute miles you will be there in four hours and that is what I was trying to do.

The remarkable thing is I trained much better for my second Dublin marathon but only ran four minutes faster in the end – 4 hours 17 as against 4 hours 21. I remember at mile 18 wanting to stop. I was saying to myself I had done this kind of time in the last marathon so what was the point. I wasn't going to make my target. I was doing well over nine-minute miles at that stage. Fortunately, my friend Aideen came along then and ran the next ten miles with me, talking me through them.

When I finished the race I was gutted. All I wanted was to break the four hours and I knew I could have. I was at 1 hr 52 minutes at the half-marathon mark. But then of course the elation you get after a very long race kicked in and my running partner, Maura, had got in under four hours and I was glad for her and felt it was worth it. I had desperate nausea afterwards.

I kept a running diary when I was training for the marathon. I can see now when I look back on it that an injury was coming on, but I didn't see that at the time, because I didn't want to. I had little notes saying, 'Had a good run but felt a twinge', and then,' That twinge still there.' All the time I ran on it until it decided for me that I couldn't run any more.

If I had been sensible I would have said that it wasn't my year and put it off. I used to feel a pull in my ileotibial band, from my knee to my hip. It would pull first and then snap, like a bang. It stops you. You can't run. It goes into spasm. That's what happened to me at the ten-mile mark. I stopped and tried to stretch it out but had to drag myself through the rest of the marathon.

My goal at the moment is to get faster but not to do the longer distance. You do everything in your own time. I would go to any race that I can get to and there are loads around Dublin. I do 5ks, 10ks, whatever I can. I would love to do another marathon but right now I'm hoping to do my first triathlon soon. The swimming would be the hard part for me.

Ray D'Arcy

I started off doing the BUPA run, which was the one I enjoyed the least. I'd never done a 10k before and it's short so you can run fast. I started at the top where all the fast runners are and discovered that the worst thing you can do is take off like a bullet out of the gun. It's soul-destroying having people pass you all the time.

With half- and full marathons you know you'll settle into your eight-minute-mile groove or whatever pace it is you run at. You also know you're likely to hook up with somebody who'll run the course with you. So the longer runs are really good for letting you pull back in again whenever you feel up to it.

But I didn't enjoy the Dublin marathon. I had done the training, building up gradually over the summer and increasing my mileage. You're supposed to get 3 x 20 miles in before the event, according to the programme I was following, but I only got 2 x 20 miles and a couple of 17.5 runs in, all which I suffered after. But then I would be fine the next day. It had been calculated I should run it in 3.37 or 3.38 or so.

But the marathon experience was completely different. The only thing I can think of is that during the jostling for position at the beginning I did something to my legs. Because 10 miles in I got this really bad pain in my upper left thigh. I was 16 miles in and then the whole mental thing kicked in with suggestions coming into my head like, 'I don't recognise this feeling,' and, 'What's this discomfort?'

I would have known from my own runs that for a couple of miles it would be tough. But then I expected to get into a rhythm where I would have this lovely 15 miles or so behind me and still be enjoying it, before having to suffer at the end. But it didn't work out that way.

At the 10 miles I completely gave up the idea that I would get in anywhere near my target time. I kept moving. My half-marathon time was really poor, five to six minutes over, at 1.45/1.46. Then at 20 miles it was 2.40 and that was pretty good. I had an hour to do the last six miles and that's what it took me.

I was feeling horrible. There was a couple of times at the water station where I came down to a walk. Then this angel called Derek arrived somewhere around Ballsbridge when we had about three or four miles to go. I don't know his full story but he had hoped to do it in three hours and something happened along the way. He said he had jet-lag but he was still full of energy compared to everyone else; we were like the walking dead.

He spotted me anyway and we struck up a conversation. I told him I needed to get in in 3.40 and he said I'd have to make the effort to do that. So he shouted encouragement and ran with me. He did everything bar push me over the line. He said his hope of doing it in three hours was long gone so he might as well do something worthwhile. I did 3.41 in the end.

I did find the people along the sidelines were brilliant. It's an interesting study. You start off and everybody is happy, happy, chatting, chatting. For the first 15 miles it's OK until you go over to the southside. Then the thing moves on and everybody gets more and more silent. Everyone reverts into their own little hell.

I had to wear insoles because in my training I was getting all sorts of pain, and shin splints. They seemed to be working. I spotted a guy in Bermuda shorts and a pair of leisure shoes on the start line of the marathon and thought, 'Someone should be there to stop this kind of thing!'

On my previous BUPA run I met a guy who was also running in Dublin as a marathon virgin. There was a picture of him afterwards in *The Irish Times* and he looked grey – not a good look. If you're not fit it can be so hard. I've seen guys in real hardship, their bodies flailing all around the place.

After the marathon Jenny saw me and said she was scared by how I looked. It really knocks you for six. I had done the required training for a novice so I hadn't been ill-prepared.

Even when I go out and do maybe 10 miles now, I think how the hell did I ever do 26 miles. It was never a case for me of finishing the marathon and then wanting to get out and do another one. I'll probably go back to doing triathlons because there's more variety and fun in it.

I suppose when you look back on it, it's like most things in life. The more distance you get from it, the greater your sense of achievement.

Gerry Galvin

The competitive element was there for me since 1995 when my half-marathons started going down to one and a half hours. After that it became all about personal bests. It was definitely hard work up to then because we were only ever doing 10-mile training sessions before the half-marathon. But then we upped it to 15 miles and that made a half-marathon an absolute walk in the park, once you go over the mileage. If you could run 30 miles comfortably, a marathon would be a doddle, but you don't do that. The body gives out after mile 20.

The body has to be in fantastic condition if you're going to be doing half-marathons as part of your training and 20 miles on a Sunday. The engine has to be working perfectly or else you're going to be stuck.

I wouldn't recommend anyone to be given a year's notice to run a very high-profile marathon like the London event, as happened with me. By all means do it for a lesser profile one but it is so difficult to get into London and we got in only because of three cancellations. There are 120,000 applicants for 40,000 places. It is one of the most prestigious marathons in the world at the moment because you finish at a palace, Buckingham Palace. You don't know where you finish in New York or Moscow but in London, you run along the Thames, it's designed that you run on flyovers and bridges where people are running over your head and you can actually clock your time by this. You know that you're at the half-marathon stage and that they're three-quarters way around for instance. London is such a colourful marathon and the crowds are fantastic. Every year that goes by it gets more prestigious and to get my place in 1992 was probably a waste because it could have been a better time for me.

If you finish London in three hours and have a certificate for that, you will readily be accepted into other major marathon events such as in New York, based upon your personal best in a London marathon. Also London attracts the top stars and that means you have television coverage so there's the possibility you might even be seen in a marathon. Dublin doesn't have television coverage. There aren't enough high-profile runners there to attract it; the sponsors aren't there.

I tried afterwards to get into London and couldn't get in on my own. If you want to get in with charities you have to raise a lot of money and we didn't have the time for it. You can also book places through a hotel in London but you have to pay extortionate prices to do it and stay in that hotel. The only other way is if you're an elite athlete, running in under two and a half hours, or maybe if you're Ethiopian and you're winning world championships. There's usually about 10,000 of the elite, then some of the Special Forces, the hippos and the chickens and all those. They get in as a charity. So there's 30,000 places left after that and it's a pure lottery if you get in.

It took me 4 hours 32 minutes to do that first London marathon in 1992 and I was in bed for four days after it. I was extremely bad with everything: knee pains, leg pains. All the joints were affected; the ankles were sore, all the muscles. I probably didn't rehydrate correctly either. It was purely that I was a novice and ill-prepared. I didn't have the miles clocked up. The maximum I had done was 14 miles. Up to the half-way point I was OK, but I walked the last five miles.

No matter how ill-prepared you are, you will complete a city marathon as opposed to the ones in the countryside or remote areas, because of the people and the surroundings, the cars, the buzz, the music. They all bring you home. Also your perception of the route, psychologically, gives you the impression you're only going around in a circle and you'll finish in the city, unlike when you're running out in the country, over a motorway, or over a river. Where are you going to turn to come back is all you're thinking of.

You do become wise after one or two marathons on the way you hydrate yourself before a marathon and if you follow the rules it does work. You know you're going to have water stations along the way. So if you hydrate properly and go to the toilet maybe an hour before the race and then maybe again five minutes beforehand, you shouldn't have to worry again unless you have stomach cramps or something like that you can't allow for.

Before a marathon you try to eliminate all problems that surround your life. Everything should be perfect as regards your family, your work, body, your shoes, your running gear. All you should have to worry about is the route. So much of the information you get is confusing. I tend to stick to one routine that suits me, as recommended by a particular coach.

You want to be training all the time for a marathon. Once you get to the 20-mile stage in your runs, you start eating into energy reserves that have never been used before. You lose essential elements in your body and it takes an awful long time for them to replenish. They reckon it takes months to get them back into your body. That's why after a marathon it's important to take things slowly and to build back up gradually.

I had a week's rest after the Dublin marathon last year and then did a 10k run ten minutes faster than ever before. But I wasn't fit to walk for two days afterwards. I had built up so much back into my muscles and then the whole lot burnt out.

The week before a marathon is the hardest part for any amateur or professional, because you have to do so little mileage. Psychologically you think you're interfering with your performance because you're reducing your mileage. But if you have your work done, you're following a programme, you're happy and you've no injuries, the last week should be rest. You've got to be able to build up the reserves for that journey. It's a long, long way. When you're at 20 miles you can ask yourself how many other people could run that. It's about 1% of a given group anywhere. Many have run half-marathons and 10ks but the marathon is an elite area.

You have to be mentally and physically right for it or you'll end up doing some serious damage and maybe kill yourself. You take a risk running a marathon. People have died running them, or even on half-marathons.

I was running here all the time and then got talking to Gerry Thomas, ex-Dublin runner, one of the best in the country, who coached us for the last Dublin marathon. When you're running with someone good your times get better. But I found the Dublin marathon in 2006 a lot harder than previous years because of the fact I put a lot more into it. I'd say I was definitely down on time because I was out of routine. Number one, I didn't have the fuel because I was having a breakfast and then a banana and yoghurt at 11 o'clock for the race at midday.

I hit the wall for the last six miles or so. I completely slowed down to a jogging rate. The pains moved up my legs. I felt restricted and then little cramps, little tremors, were coming towards the end. I was trying to push myself and then we entered Ballsbridge and there was such a wind it was like trying to run against someone pushing you. Then I started getting very thirsty and needed rehydrating. The last water station was at 24 miles and I had two miles to do. I had to stop and have a full bottle of water. I stopped to do that and then I kept going again. You are warned that at 24 miles it's the last water station because of all the people around, and to load up and take as much fluid as possible.

I built right back up and for the last 500 yards I sprinted to the line and then ran out of steam. Once I got the water in and the cramps out I was OK. There's a trick to getting rid of leg cramps. You have to stop and put your leg right back underneath you and the other one completely forward. You're literally pulling the muscles back into your leg. It hurts but it's over in a minute. It untangles everything. At that stage all I wanted to do was finish.

If you ever get a stitch when you're running it can be very hard to get rid of it. Sod's law you'll get it running into a hill. You blow through your lips as hard as you can when you're breathing out. That is the trick of the trade. Literally, make your lips blue and then you feel the whole thing dissipating.

At the finish, I lost my concentration, I was rambling. I wasn't with it. I wouldn't have been able to answer many questions after it. I was doing well to stand up. I was trying to keep myself upright and I didn't want to collapse. But I didn't want any questions from anybody because I would have had to use up the last bit of energy I wanted to take my time to focus and I was OK then.

Because of the training I had done I recovered quickly though. At 12 o'clock I finished and at 4 o'clock I was shopping. The funny thing was I was late for the train then so that after a marathon I had to run for the train to get back to Westport. After 26 miles I had to race down the track, limping more than running. I made it anyway.

Mary Kennedy

I did my first marathon in 1981 and it took me 3 hours 40 minutes to finish, which wasn't bad. I was very fit then. When I ran it again, 20 years later, it took me 4 hours 20 minutes to complete. The only thing prior to that that was as physically testing was having my first baby.

I remember training for the 1981 event. I followed a fitness regime in the *RTÉ Guide* by Noel Carroll. The first ever Dublin City Marathon was in 1979 and the advice I was following was for the 1981 event. I had started part-time as a continuity announcer and was straight out of college. Noel had devised a regime for someone training from zero to a marathon in six months. I cut it out and picked up the training from the level of fitness I was at and followed it to the letter. It really worked. Marathon training isn't awful hard but you do have to be very disciplined. You never actually ran a marathon before the marathon. You do only one 20-mile run. Maybe once a week for three or four weeks you might do 15 miles. But it is the cumulative effect of gradually building up the mileage that works. It pays off.

I remember my mother worrying that I was pushing myself too hard when I was so young. She was of a generation that didn't do any formal fitness regime like that. She worked in the Civil Service and they used to cycle to Wexford for two weeks' holidays every summer, so they were actually fit. I had to hide the level of training I was doing from her and used to sneak out for my 18-mile runs with the dog, who would collapse for the rest of the day. My mother would wonder what was wrong with the animal. Was she dying?

I love setting myself challenges and going for the marathon was a real challenge. It was also such a novelty back then. There was the same buzz about it as there is now with the women's mini-marathon.

When I did it again in 2000 that was enough. I don't like competitions now and will stick to running for fun from now on.

You know, running isn't supposed to be all pleasant. You have to realise it's about pushing yourself. There is nothing wrong with feeling bits of pain, shortness of breath, or having thoughts going through your head like, 'I wish this was over,' because it will be over. On your 30-minute run you tell yourself you can last the half-hour. After that, when it is over, you will feel great about yourself.

I've done the women's mini-marathon twice, fund raising for my African trip. I do think there is a great sense of self apparent in the women who run it. A lot of them would have done nothing like that before and then realise, 'I can do this.' Neighbours of mine say 'Aren't you great running it,' and I tell them, 'Sure you could do it as well.'

I've done the Aran Islands half-marathon too and would love to go to Inis Mór and do it again. It's so lovely there. The scenery is fabulous. You go from the airstrip at Cill Ronáin into the village to the top of the island. The women have tea and sandwiches outside their houses for you. I like to do whatever events I can for charity because you feel you are doing it for a reason.

Professor Risteárd Mulcahy

I went off running for six months once because of a soft-tissue injury to the knee. I had an X-Ray and of course X-Rays always show up arthritis. I had grave doubts about that so I got a second opinion from a radiologist who was a sports specialist. He looked at my X-Ray and then at my knee and said the best thing for you is to go back running.

I started by doing a few 10ks at first. I was soon averaging about five to eight miles a day, sometimes more, and seldom less than five miles. I was running four to five times a week, any time that I could, morning or evening. I was very busy all the time so I could run at six in the morning, get home, shower and have my breakfast and be in the hospital for half past eight. Or I could run when I came back in the evening.

Running is extreme, especially running a half- or full marathon. The first Dublin marathon was a killer for me because I didn't train adequately and I 'hit the wall' and all that went with it. The second Dublin marathon I trained a little bit better but only took five minutes off my time. For my third and last marathon in Belfast I went out to Wicklow for two weeks beforehand and spent my time running up and down the mountains. Even though I was 63 at the time, I took 30 minutes off my best time. I did the Belfast marathon in 3 hours 50 minutes which for my age was good. I had been taking 4 hours 20 minutes up to that. That was by dint of proper training.

Mary Walsh

I did my first 10k in 2001 and after that ran a couple of half-marathons, including the Louisburgh to Westport one, which is flat and lovely. A friend I used to run with in Galway said she would do a marathon. I was seeing a lot of runners at work and had travelled to the Chicago Marathon in 2001 as a physiotherapist with Croí. It was a great experience and I decided then to do New York myself as a runner.

In November 2002 I arrived in New York for the marathon and found myself asking, 'What am I doing here? I am a sham.' The day before I spent walking around New York thinking negative thoughts and feeling I should go home, even though I had done the training. Maybe it was because I was a bit tired from the flight and there was the whole day before spent at an exposition about the marathon. Fortunately I woke up on the day of the event and felt, 'I can do this.'

The problem with the New York marathon is that you're hanging around for a good while before it starts and in November it's cold. There are two million spectators and 35,000 runners. The whole route is lined with people. We wore Irish singlets so people knew where we were from. I remember hearing lots of 'Come on Ireland!' It's fascinating too because the route passes through the different boroughs of New York, the Jewish area, Harlem, the Bronx, Brooklyn and so on.

I had trained up to 20 miles and remember telling myself at mile six that it was like starting my 20-mile training run then. That's how I dealt with it. I remember at mile 16 getting a bit tired and meeting up with a friend. It's the only quiet part of the race before you turn on to First Avenue which goes on for four miles. The crowds are roaring all along. It was really hard from mile 22. At that stage I was telling myself, 'Look, you've often done four miles when you're tired or off form so do it now too. You're only wrecked. There's nothing else wrong with you. It'll only take you as long as a half-hour TV programme. This too will pass.' So I never stopped.

Altogether I have run three marathons and there have been only 38 seconds between my times, which were all around 3 hours 44 minutes.

It's a funny feeling at the end. You are delighted but you're too wrecked to enjoy it because you have no energy. It's a real deep kind of self-contentment and then elation comes after it. We celebrated later that night. When you have done it as part of a group there's a real high talking about it. It doesn't matter if your time was two hours or six hours. You've all achieved the same thing. If you are against anybody you are against yourself and nobody else.

I realised I couldn't really remember the first marathon. Just 10 minutes of it were clear in my mind. But the second one in 2004 was imprinted on my mind. It was really hot, around 24 degrees. I went out much faster but the last six miles took me longer and I really struggled. I told myself to keep running because I knew I was better off not to walk or stop.

Afterwards I knew I'd put my body through the mill. I had five cold-sores within two days and was completely worn out. I didn't enjoy it as much. I couldn't wait to get back to the cold and the wet. I was too hot and couldn't hydrate myself. The experience put me off marathons but not running. Training for a marathon is so extreme. I would lose maybe a stone in weight. It suits some people fine but takes its toll on others.

I never train more than four days – up to 40 miles a week – for a marathon, although I would do some hill-walking maybe on another day.

I've done some wonderful half-marathons since which I really enjoyed, the Connemara and Aran Islands event. Pádraig Ó Céide does a fanstastic job with the one on Inis Mór. It's a class run. You go for the weekend, stay in a B&B out there if you like. Nearly all the locals have a water stand outside their houses for you. There's a lovely meal on the Saturday night. You raise money for the Children's Hospital in Crumlin so it's all in a good cause. There's a beautiful run out in Daingean in Galway too, where you're going by the water the whole way.

When I did decide to run New York a third time in the 2006 marathon, my goal was to finish it in four hours. Unfortunately, I didn't feel my training had gone too well and I got bored with the long runs. I wasn't really sure how it would go but in the end it was the one I enjoyed most. I went out slowly because I was afraid of hitting the wall. I also ran with someone I knew for 23 miles which made it so much easier. I felt good at the end. I had a bit of gas left in the tank. I felt really strong. So I learned that the best thing to do is go out slow.

I've finished now doing marathons. Well, I might do one in a couple of years but no more for now.

8

RUNNERS ON RUNNING AND AGEING

Ernie Caffrey

You can read all you like about how you're supposed to be as you get older but it's the way you feel that counts. When I do a training session I have no discomfort. I feel perfectly fit. So while I feel that way I'll continue with it.

I do feel I'm doing myself a good turn in regard to ageing. Now they tell you that you can overdo it but I wouldn't train if I was tired or if I felt I was in any way forcing myself. If I'm tired I relax, lie down and go to bed. I won't train. I think one of the worst things is to force yourself to do things because you think you should be doing them. If you keep injury-free it doesn't knock that much out of you.

You are much more in tune with your body when you're training. Your muscular development improves, in contrast to what normally happens as people get older and their muscles atrophy and go saggy. I took up the shot-putt too and got the silver for that in Nenagh. That's what I mean about it all helping your muscular development. I also play golf, which is my sport of choice. I'm not focused on the game but I'll hit a round. I don't want to do too much, though, because there isn't the time. I'll stay running as long as I enjoy it and keep fit.

I would recommend running or at least a good exercise regime for everybody. I think the Health Services Executive would get by with a lot less money if more people were fitter and gave up smoking. Competitive running wouldn't suit most people but a fitness regime of a moderate nature would be good for anyone.

The running seems to have an uplifting effect on life too. I would think it would be good for people with depression because it takes your mind off worldly things in a way. You're concentrating on what you're doing and looking forward to reaching the end of the run. You're not thinking of dying anyway, which is a help!

Grainne Cunningham

I would love to think I'll be running into my sixties and seventies. It is so powerful to be fit and to tap into your body. When you start to realise the right things to do with your body you see there is so far to go. It's the best drug you can get.

Gerry Galvin

I can't see myself stopping running in the near or distant future. I find that when you're doing marathons the average age of people running around you is 45. Count how many young people run a marathon. When you see them congregating outside they're all getting older. You never retire from running unless you have an injury. It's something that you keep going all the time and that you can take up at a later stage. You don't have to start at 21. You can start at 41. You're born to run. It's not something you have to acquire skills for and it's recommended by all the health experts in that it's a very good form of aerobic exercise.

Obviously if you're smoking or unfit it may not be for you. It's up to everyone if they want to take it on but I can't think of anyone it would not be suited to. If you have physical disabilities you can't do it, but people with transplants, asthmatics, diabetics, people with various conditions, they all run. You can adapt yourself to run, so there should be very few people who can't take it up.

Fortunately, my own health is sound. I have full body sports massages maybe every two months and find them a great help.

You have to have rest periods. I do a small bit of swimming. I would have one night where I relax and sauna. I'm always stretching. I'd be stretching at Mass nearly. Fortunately the nature of my work is that I'm moving all the time. So that helps with the preparation and the warm-up. It's labour-intensive work and you are moving a lot so you don't need a lot of motivation to go for a run after it because you're warming up since 10 o'clock.

I'd spend maybe 20 minutes at home warming up too. I'd have the kids with me in the room stretching as well, maybe swinging underneath me. Laura, two and a half, she'd be doing a stretch up against the radiator.

My worst nightmare with my running would be the an injury or breakage. You lose your fitness over a few weeks. I suppose if you have the running in your blood and you're enthusiastic, you would find some way around it. There are prosthetics if you need them.

Dr Mick Loftus

People say to me, you're crazy working so hard at your age, but I enjoy it. I'd be lost sitting up there in the house. We're definitely an ageist society and I blame the older people as much for that because they ask why should they do things, because of their age. The 2006 National Council for Ageing and Older people slogan 'Say No to Ageism' was great – if only you could get people to think that way. But even if older people do go to gyms, they are made to feel the odd one out because of this ageist society. So older people unfortunately complain all the time of having a pain here or a pain there or that their blood pressure is up.

I have no problems with sleep. As soon as my head hits the pillow I'm gone. So many older people are on sedatives to sleep. If we could only get them into exercise. There are so many things they could be doing. If you could get them going in the thirties and forties and keep them going.

I go into some of the nursing homes and it's sad to see so many of them sitting around doing no activity. You think they could have avoided that if only they'd taken exercise.

There are so many sporting facilities developed now. They're well used when fellows are playing football but then they finish. There's a lot of money invested in these facilities but they need to be used and to be used continuously.

I never think of getting old. I know I am getting older but it doesn't come into my mind. I'm as good today as I was 30 years ago or whenever you like and I think it's being fit that keeps me that way.

When I meet my peers and they say you look so good, how do you do it, again I don't think that way. A lot of women put on too much weight in the forties, I know it's difficult for mothers with babies. I can understand that but when they get older, that's the time of life to get into the exercise.

I know a lot of older people play golf now, which is good. The only thing is that golf is not as intense. People hit the ball and then they stand. You want to keep it going. People strike the ball, walk up and stand and wait for someone to hit the other one. They need to keep moving but it's hard to get that message across.

I see women and men out walking. They stroll, but they tell you they go for a walk every day. For the benefits to accrue they need to be walking faster. When they're not fit they think they're getting short of breath and that something is wrong. Naturally when I start running, first I get out of breath but then after a while I'm fine.

The odd time I give a spurt. I say, here goes, if I'm going up a hill. I sprint that way. My son Michael has a runner, a treadmill. I go on that sometimes, very fast, and maybe keep it up for five or six minutes, maybe slowing it down again for a bit. I'm not preparing for anything; it's about feeling good and staying healthy.

Workwise, no matter what you do, you seem to be able to do it all better. I would even go so far as to say that if someone dies in a family, the people left behind would be able to tackle those kinds of things better when they're fit. Even for depression I would say it helps. You know, when people are a bit down in themselves, it's great for them to get out to take exercise.

The age I am this year, 78, doesn't bother me at all. Death never occurs to me, because I feel fit. It's going to happen anyway. Edie and I are celebrating fifty years married this year.

I'm looking forward to my eightieth birthday. I've nothing planned. Maybe I'll climb that mountain out in India, whatever it's called! Ah no, I hope to keep doing what I'm doing.

Professor Risteárd Mulcahy

I did a few 10ks after the marathons up until my hip operation in 1994. When I walked I was getting pain and it was limiting my mobility. The operation was a great success but I stopped running because I didn't want to damage my new hip, which has been perfect ever since the operation 13 years ago. I stopped running but I started walking and I also cycle and play golf in Portmarnock, which is quite a tough course. So I'm still very active all the time.

Every time I see a nice athletic person running today I get a certain longing for it again. I think my hip trouble was caused by twisting around at squash. My orthopaedic surgeon wasn't too enthusiastic about my going running again.

I was six feet but I've lost two inches. The spongy intervertebral discs atrophy slowly with age, like your muscles. As they atrophy they get thinner so somebody like me will lose height.

If I hadn't the hip trouble I could probably have continued jogging. I always did around the same speed, about 7.5 miles per hour. I settled down at that. Obviously if I had run into my eighties I would have been running at a slower rate. That would be normal.

From the time I started doing my research work in 1961 I was always interested in exercise. We had installed our first big heart unit in St Vincent's Hospital and I was in charge of it. I had a huge library of medical books there that covered the whole physiology of exercise. I used to write a lot for the newspapers about the value of being physically active. It reduces your risk of heart disease and high blood pressure and redresses the risk of colon, breast and prostate cancer. It relieves osteoarthritis and may also be beneficial to conditions like asthma.

One of the sad things about sedentary people is that they don't realise the huge joy to be had from using your body properly. It's not just your muscular-skeleton that benefits but your overall body functions as well.

I believe that people who exercise a lot get huge advantages both physically and particularly psychologically. When you're involved in exercise, you're in closer contact with nature and society. One of the things I loved when I ran in races was the people I met. You could get on to fairly intimate social contact with men and women you were running with because there was great social contact with it.

It's all summed up by the saying: there's no joy without suffering. If you want to sit down and enjoy company and have a pint or two of Guinness, it's better if you do it after a run, because if you knew you had to go for a run after your few drinks, that would ruin it. A lot of people who run never become competitive but when you think we have 10,000 people running in a marathon, it's big business now.

There is no age limit to physical exercise, as long as the exercise is done within the limits of your physical powers and your psychological and mental powers, as these play a great role. The very fact of fear of exercise will limit people very much. Some people think it's dangerous and doctors and the medical profession have a very bad history in the way they've been so negative about exercise.

It's only lately that even the heart people are beginning to realise that their patients should become physically active. We have strong evidence that aerobic exercise, which improves lung and heart fitness, stabilises the very delicate lining of the arteries. You are therefore much less liable to get clots or cholesterol deposits and things.

You probably live longer too if you're active rather than inactive, but what is very important is you're much less likely to have a period of disability or loss of independence before you die. This is the great benefit of exercise. My wife teaches old people who are in chairs to do exercise. They're all religious people, old nuns and old priests. They never took any exercise because the Church was opposed to anything that might promote a body culture. Being proud of your body was associated with sex. It's curious. The Church was unfortunately an inhibiting factor for many people. If you started talking about how much you enjoyed your body, the health of your body and the activity of it, that would be frowned upon.

I hope to continue exercising into the future as I am currently doing. I do have to reduce now. I'm even finding going around Portmarnock with the electric caddy car is too much for me so I have a caddy now. But you have to accept these adaptations that are necessary. I will probably have to say to my golf friends soon that I only want to play nine holes. I first took up golf in hospital but gave it up for the 25 years I was playing squash and running. I play 18 holes still these days and run around the course like anybody else and still play to a handicap of 18.

I think you should keep on exercising as long as you can. A lot of the people I see for stress tests are in their seventies and have been doing no exercise. But they can become fit even at the age of 75 as long as they go about it properly. Once you start exercising aerobically or for flexibility you are slowing the normal attrition that occurs with age.

9

STARTING A RUNNING PROGRAMME

HOW TO BEGIN RUNNING

The first thing to remember when you start a running programme is not to push yourself too hard. Even though running is a natural movement for most of us, it takes a lot of practice before anyone can run very far. The best way to start out any exercise programme is to build up gradually. The old adage 'walk before you can run' is one that must be heeded, as the first step to running is indeed walking.

Depending on your level of fitness, you may be able to walk five miles without difficulty or only a mile with great difficulty. The important thing is to start from your own level and then add bits to that on a day-to-day or week-to-week basis.

So if you have a regular one-mile walking route that you like, begin by running the odd 200- or 300-metre stretch along the way. Do this a few times until the activity becomes comfortable, then challenge yourself to run a little further each time.

Becoming a runner is all about setting regular goals and making the effort to achieve them. Your focus should be on building up longer distances before considering working on your speed. The body needs to be able to handle the strain of long runs on muscles and joints before it can put them under increased pressure with speed training. After three months you should know if running is for you. Here are some running tips:

- Don't run before you can walk. Always start by walking before speeding up into a run.
- Make sure to always wear comfortable trainers and light, loose clothing when exercising to avoid any pressure on the body.
- Take your age into account as well as your medical history. You should not attempt to run if you suffer from breathing, heart or blood difficulties.
- Always remember to warm up and cool down. Begin slow and finish slow.
- Assess how flexible your body is. Have you been active or sedentary of late? Do you feel stiff when you walk or exercise? Are your ankle, knee and hip joints mobile, strong and flexible? Don't begin running unless your body feels up to the challenge. Ligaments need constant stretching. Age and lack of use can reduce their function, shortening your stride when you run and leaving you open to injury.
- Attack small hills quickly and for longer inclines, approach in a relaxed tempo.
- A good running technique will ensure you perform to the best of your abilities.
- Focus on having a relaxed style.
- Make sure your shoulders are loose and not hunched up.
- Keep your back straight.
- Try to keep your head up and facing forward.
- Keep hands cupped, but not balled up into fists.
- Use arms like pistons to propel. Increase movement

when you need to dig deep for going up hills or sprinting. The angle of your arms to your body should remain at 90 degrees.

- Lift your knees enough to lift your hips at each footfall.
- Land on your heel and roll up to the toes with each step.
- Young bodies enjoy fast cell renewal whereas older bodies regenerate at a slower rate. Just remember to keep running at the level you feel capable of at all times and don't overdo it. Regular training will keep you fit into old age.
- Some people enjoy their own company and prefer to exercise alone, while others need other runners around them. Decide at the outset whether you need companions, and if you do, treat them as 'training buddies' to keep you exercising and motivated. Running may seem like a fun pastime at the start but over time, the novelty may fade. You need to make running a regular feature in your life in order to keep going with it.
- A proper training programme involves working out until you feel tired, followed by rest, then training that bit harder the next time to achieve further progress. The rest period is as important as the training because the body needs time to recover from strenuous exertion. If you fail to rest, you will pay for it eventually as the body suffers injury or decline and then demands a long rest period.
- A normal pulse rate for a man is 72 beats a minute, 80 for women. However, pulse rates vary from morning

to night and can go up and down in response to the level of activity in hand. Given that the heart is a muscle, it too becomes bigger and stronger with exercise. The fitter you are, the lower your resting pulse (best taken when you wake up).

- Good running is dependent on good oxygen intake. The process of taking in oxygen makes demands on the chest, lungs, heart and blood system. Training at high altitudes helps increase oxygen intake.

- Eat something light around two hours before your run. Drink plenty of water to make sure you are sufficiently hydrated.

- Allow for good days and bad days. The body is often likened to a machine but its performance can vary from day to day and, indeed, hour to hour.

- It's fine to breathe through the mouth when running as you may be going too fast to breathe through the nose. Take long, deep breaths if you feel a stitch coming on.

- Try and keep your inner dialogue positive as you run. Tell yourself you can meet the challenge you've set yourself. Don't listen to that voice urging you to stop.

- Big, firm muscles help the body move along easily and quickly. The bigger your muscles the more energy you use up each day, even while resting. One pound of muscle uses up 35 calories a day to function, in contrast to one pound of fat which needs one or two calories. Fat contains more than twice as much energy as carbohydrate but requires more oxygen intake for it to be used as an energy fuel. After 30 minutes or so of running, glycogen stores in the muscles become depleted and fat is then drawn on for energy.

- Some people are built naturally for speed, others for endurance. The balance of slow-twitch and fast-twitch muscles in your body will determine the type of runner you can be.

- For increased muscle power in the legs, do hill-running. For strong chest muscles, go swimming. A balanced weight-training programme for arms, legs and torso will counteract weaknesses and improve athletic performance overall.

- Don't push yourself further than your body can go in its current state. You will need to proceed with a certain level of care, depending on your age and background.

- If you are obese, as opposed to overweight, extra precautions have to be taken. Start off by walking. If you are simply overweight, support your new exercise regime with a healthy diet, walking at first, and when you feel ready to run, go for it.

- Try running on soft surfaces, such as grass or sand, before going on cement or tarmac.

- If you've been ill, you really need to go slowly at first. If you feel any soreness or strain in your leg muscles after a run, take a day off. For best practice, alternate exercise days with rest days. Make sure on rest days to remain active around the home and at work, thereby keeping your metabolism boosted.

- Training with other people can sometimes mean you have to run faster to keep up all the time. It's important to have sessions where you move at a pace that suits you too every now and again. You'll probably find you enjoy these runs more than others.

- Remember to cut yourself some slack every now and again. If you're chugging away at a training schedule and feel yourself becoming stale, simply stop for a while. Taking a complete break for a few days can do you the world of good.

- Within a few weeks of taking up a running regime, many people will be able to keep running for 20 to 30 minutes, covering two to three miles in the process. If you can perform this workout three our four times a week, you will have achieved a good level of fitness.

- Some people swear by stretches as a key warm-up routine while others prefer to leave them for the finish. Do whatever suits you best. For a warm-up or cool down, begin with brisk walking for five minutes or so before engaging in some gentle stretches. Stretch the muscles in the calves, thighs and back and swing your arms high and wide. There are special stretches suitable for runners and most gyms carry demonstration charts. Alternatively, consult with other runners to find out the best stretches pre- and post-workout.

10

A 5k Running Programme

GETTING STARTED

Start out by aiming to run one minute at a time, without stopping. Plan to increase your running time from one minute to two minutes, gradually working up to 20-minute and then 30-minute runs. Ideally, for a maintenance fitness programme, you will be able to run for 30 minutes three times a week. You should train on alternate days, giving yourself one long two-day break during the week, probably at the weekend. A typical schedule could include running on Monday, Wednesday and Friday, with Saturday and Sunday off.

For somebody who has never really run properly before, running for a whole minute can prove exhausting. It may indeed prove so challenging as to put you off running for life. But this is where tenacity and perseverance are called for. Resolve to stick with your new training regime, no matter how difficult. The beauty of running is that with consistent practice, it does become easier. The more you do, the more you can do.

If you have health problems or physical disabilities that make it impossible to achieve running goals, you shouldn't entertain the idea in the first place. However, for most of us who follow a six-week beginner's training programme similar to the one outlined here, running for 30 minutes without a break is achievable.

GOAL: TO RUN FOR 30 MINUTES (5K)
AFTER SIX WEEKS FROM TAKING UP RUNNING

Week 1
Allot three 30-minute sessions this week for your running training – ideally on alternate days. You can train on a treadmill at a gym or outdoors, whichever you prefer.

Session 1
Complete this sequence as often as you can:

Walk for one minute, run for one minute.

If you find the running very difficult, you may be going too fast. Try to jog for the 60-second period, taking it nice and steady. If you need more than a minute to recover from the running, that's fine. Just be sure to start running again as soon as you can, at intervals throughout the half-hour.

Note
If you are seriously overweight and lead a sedentary life, commence with a walking programme instead of a running programme. Allot the same 30 minutes three times a week to working out. As walking is an easier exercise, you should be able to increase the regularity of your walks up to 30 minutes a day by the end of six weeks. You will enjoy similar positive results of improved physical fitness and muscle tone, weight loss and enhanced wellbeing. You may then feel ready to introduce running into your training, adhering to the programme here.

Session 2

Follow the same one-minute run/walk routine and if you feel up to it, extend the running period for a little longer each time.

Session 3

As for Session 2, except that if you have been allowing yourself to take walking breaks longer than your running bursts in the previous two sessions, stop it now. You are no longer a beginner.

Tell yourself it's good to push the body a bit harder each time. You're aiming for a goal that most people should be able to achieve in a six-week period. By the end of week 1 and session 3, try to manage some two-minute non-stop runs. You know you can.

Week 2

Allot three 30-minute sessions for your training again this week.

- Session 1: aim to run and walk at two-minute intervals.
- Session 2: aim to run a little bit longer than you walk at each interval. For example, run for three minutes and walk for two minutes, repeating to the end.
- Session 3: as for Session 2.

Note

Week 2 can prove especially trying for beginner runners as that inner voice becomes ever louder and more negative!

It is more important than ever now that you remind yourself of your goal. You must stick at this for six weeks. It's not a very long time. You can do it. You will be pleased as punch at the end when you achieve the result. You can and will run for 30-minutes non-stop. You will keep going.

Week 3

Allot three 30-minute training sessions again this week. Your aim this week is to build your running time to more than five minutes. To keep you motivated, perhaps you could add a treat such as running to music or time your treadmill session to coincide with a TV programme you can watch on the gym monitor.

- Session 1: run for three minutes or as long as you can without a break. You should find that you can easily keep running for a minute now. You have it in your legs. Keep going past two minutes, then three minutes, up to four and five minutes if possible. Walk for two minutes after you run. By the end of the session, try to have achieved an eight-minute run.
- Session 2: as for Session 1, including at least two eight-minute runs. You can do it.
- Session 3: go all out for this last session of the week. Begin running and keep going for as long as you can. If you need to stop after five minutes, do so, walk for two minutes, then start again. Aim to run for more than ten minutes in one go. Ideally, you should finish week 3 having completed one 15-minute run. You're half-way there!

Week 4

Now that you've come this far, be sure not to give in. By now, you should be reaping some of the many benefits that come with regular aerobic exercise. The scales may show that you've lost a pound or two. Already you may that notice your clothes fit you better, as excess fat is burnt away. Your mood may have lifted. You probably feel better about yourself, happier that you are using your body beneficially and pushing yourself physically and mentally to perform in this new and challenging way.

- Session 1: run for as long as you possibly can without stopping. Be sure to keep going for at least 15 minutes – the end-goal for week 3. Then keep going some more, up to 20 minutes if you can. Rest and then run for a few minutes more, again for as long as you can. Really push yourself. You're doing great.
- Session 2: this session is all about trying to repeat the performance of session 1, which may seem too much to ask. But the body adapts readily to change and rises to meet new challenges. You can do this. Keep running for at least 20 minutes.
- Session 3: as for Session 2.

Week 5

You're nearly there now, with two weeks to go. You've advanced from being a non-runner to someone who can keep running non-stop for at least 20 minutes. Who would ever have thought it! Your goal this week is to maintain progress.

- Session 1: run for 10 minutes, walk for one minute. Repeat this set twice more.
- Session 2: run for as long as you can, up to 20 minutes; walk for up to five minutes; run the last five minutes.
- Session 3: as for session 1.

Week 6

You've made it to the last week. You're still running and you can vary your runs from 10 minutes to 20 minutes as you choose. This is a major achievement. This week you need to add another 10 minutes to your longest run. You will do this during session 3. Gear yourself up for this in the first two sessions.

- Session 1: run for 15 minutes, walk for one minute. Repeat this set.
- Session 2: run for 10 minutes, walk for one minute. Repeat this set twice.
- Session 3: run and keep running until you clock up 30 minutes. You are now fit to go for your first 5k fun-run.

Well done! Of course you did it! Now that you can run for 30-minutes non-stop, the world is your oyster. The sense of achievement you will experience after completing this six-week programme should inspire you in a number of ways.

You may decide you want to build up your running talents and achieve higher goals. Go for it. If you've discovered you can actually run quite fast, you may want to explore sprinting options. It's time to inform yourself about running events, indoor and outdoor, running for fun and competitively.

Get talking to staff at your gym; invest in some of the running periodicals and magazines; explore other sporting options that may appeal to you; talk to other people you've seen running or training in ways that appeal to you. The options are endless. Whatever you decide, resolve to keep exercising. It will enhance your life and lengthen your life-span.

A 10-k Running Programme

GETTING HOOKED

You know you're hooked on running when it starts to filter into your dreams at night-time! In your mind's eye, you see yourself running at full flight, arms and legs outstretched, taking long, vigorous strides. There's a message somewhere in such dreams. You must be ready to set more ambitious goals!

Once you run your first 5k, it's natural to consider upping your running distance to the next notable milestone – 10k. On the basis that running 5k takes the average runner 30 minutes or so, with 10k you're talking about being able to keep running for a full hour or more. Working up to 60-minute non-stop runs is a gradual process, as with the initial running programme. It's a matter of conditioning your body to covering this distance and then going on to repeat the workout on a consistent basis (until you are ready for the next step – the half-marathon).

GOAL: TO RUN FOR 60 MINUTES (10K)
AFTER 12 WEEKS FROM TAKING UP RUNNING

Deciding to move up from 5k runs to 10k runs and beyond is a serious business as it confronts you with the fact that running has become an integral part of your life. You are setting real goals and preparing to follow a proper programme to achieve them. When you get to this point, it's a good time to acknowledge a new fact about yourself. You are a runner. Regular and consistent training means you have earned this title.

Once you acknowledge your runner status, you start thinking like a runner, perhaps in relation to the way you should live your life, how you should socialise, what you should eat and how big a role you should let running play in your life. It all boils down to how big a commitment you want to make to the activity, how far you want to take it and how important it is for your sense of self.

Different people take different directions at this level. Some opt to explore other sports and activities apart from running. Many people extol the virtues of triathlons, which combine running, swimming and cycling trials, loving the variety of training involved. Others sign up to focus entirely on building up their running abilities, aiming to run a half-marathon within a few months and a full marathon, perhaps, by the end of the year.

Whatever option appeals at this stage, the important thing is that you make a decision that regular, challenging, physical exercise will play a role in your life from here on. This in itself is a health plan, as it focuses on developing and improving your physical abilities.

Working out on a treadmill can be really helpful in building up your speed on a gradual basis. Being able to vary the pace is enormously helpful for monitoring progress. Interval training, where you run at high speeds for one or two minutes, before reducing to a lower speed for another minute or two, on a repeat basis, is very helpful in speed work. You'll be amazed how effective interval training like this can be. It gets easier to run faster, consistently, after these efforts. You can find through trial and error which interval sessions suit you. You may like to run hard for a full ten minutes, more slowly for five and hard again for ten. Remember:

- Be consistent with your training.
- Gradually introduce extra mileage.
- Be prepared to do one long run every week.

It suits many people to complete their long run at the weekend. With marathon training, the aim is to introduce longer distances on a gradual but consistent basis, so finishing off each week with a longer distance is an ideal foundation for starting off the new week that follows. Step up your mileage from 5k to 10k gradually over a number of weeks. This might be the basis of a six-week programme with at least three training sessions per week:

Week 1 (Week 7 from start of beginner programme)
- Session 1: 25 minutes at a nice steady pace.
- Session 2: 30 minutes steady. Aim to cover 5k.
- Take a two-day rest.
- Session 3: 35-minute run, non-stop, easy. Try to cover more than 5k.

Week 2 (four sessions)
- Session 1: run for 15 minutes, easy.
- Session 2: run for 25 minutes, steady.
- Session 3: repeat session 2.
- Take a two-day rest.
- Session 4: run for 35 minutes, trying to extend the distance covered in the previous week.

Week 3 (four sessions)
- Session 1: run for 15 minutes, easy.
- Session 2: run for 30 minutes, steady.
- Session 3: run for 25 minutes, easy.

- Session 4: run for 40 minutes, easy. Walk some of the time if you feel the need.

Week 4 (four sessions)
- Session 1: run for 20 minutes, easy.
- Session 2: run for 25 minutes, steady.
- Session 3: run for 35 minutes, steady.
- Rest two days.
- Session 4: run for 50 minutes without stopping.

Week 5 (five sessions)
- Session 1: run for 20 minutes, easy.
- Session 2: run for 25 minutes, steady.
- Session 3: run for 40 minutes, steady.
- Session 4: run for 10 minutes, easy.
- Session 5: run for 50 minutes, non-stop if possible.

Week 6 (four sessions)
- Session 1: run for 25–30 minutes, steady.
- Session 2: repeat session 1.
- Session 3: run for 10 minutes, easy.
- Session 4: Run for 60 minutes or as long as it takes you to cover 10k.

Being able to run continuously over a distance of 10k is a fantastic achievement. Half-marathons and marathons lie ahead. Once you reach 10k level all you need are another two to three months to train up to a half-marathon and two more to be able to complete your first marathon – around six to seven months training in total.

Good luck with your running dreams. Now you've come this far, be sure to keep going.

Diet, Gear and Other Practicalities

DIET

It's important to eat healthily when you begin a new running programme. Food is all about providing your body with the fuel it needs to deliver the energy required for the activities you engage in. Most women need an average 2000 calories a day to maintain a normal lifestyle while men can eat anything up to 3000 calories a day, depending on height and build. Active people obviously require additional calories to fuel their exercise. The basis of any good diet is plenty of wholegrain carbohydrates, some proteins, bare amounts of fats and little or no junk, processed or fast food. Chocolate and sweet treats should also be kept to a minimum.

Some excellent foods for the runner's diet are:

- wholewheat pasta
- brown rice
- baked beans
- wholegrain breakfast cereals
- lean red meat
- salmon and other oily fish

Remember to eat a good two hours before you go for a run, to allow adequate time for digestion.

Digestion

Not only will running improve your physique but your internal organs will benefit enormously from regular workouts. One of the biggest plusses of running is that it helps to repair dodgy digestive systems. All the movement keeps food passing through steadily so for those who suffer with sluggish bowels or constipation, running can provide immediate and consistent relief. With some people, however, things go too far in the opposite direction. The best thing is to monitor how your runs and diet affect your digestion and tweak accordingly. You can do this by keeping notes of your diet as part of your training diary. Make sure also to stay near a loo for your initial runs until the situation is under control!

Hydration

You must make sure to keep yourself well hydrated throughout your running training. Your urine should be almost clear or champagne-coloured if you are properly hydrated. Water is the best drink you could have so keep it in plentiful supply before, during and after your training and sip as required. Fizzy drinks can upset the stomach and are not good for rehydrating the body. Plain fruit juices can be very nice while specialist sports drinks are popular too – keep an eye on the calories though.

Advanced nutrition

When you get into running seriously and go out training three or four times a week, good nutrition is more important than ever. 'You are what you eat' is really one of the wisest maxims and if you liken your body to a machine you will know to feed it with good fuel to maintain good condition. Eat little and often if possible, include lots of carbohydrates, keep fats low and drink water throughout the day.

Carbohydrates are extremely important for energy and good function in aerobic exercise and the more you exert yourself, the more carboydrates you will need. Some protein and fat at each meal are also important, and immediately after exercise, you should try to eat a high-carb snack to help replenish lost glycogen stores from the muscles. Follow this up with a good meal when you get showered, changed and home again and you will feel your body thanking you for these provisions.

Eating four or five times a day does mean you have to prepare more meals but some of these can be sandwiches or maybe poached eggs so it doesn't prove too demanding. You should try to buy ingredients as fresh as possible.

Suggested meals

- Scrambled eggs on toast with beans and a pot of tea (good protein and carbs combination).
- Scrambled eggs, fish fingers and spaghetti (not too heavy).
- Boiled eggs with Ryvita and cheese and a cup of coffee (nice and light).
- Bowl of granola (oat-based) cereal with chopped walnuts, raisins, bananas and milk (high-carb and delicious).
- Wholemeal pitta bread with a variety of fillings such as cheese, red onion, iceberg lettuce, mayonnaise, chopped coriander (delicious and very convenient as a packed lunch). Alternatively, toast some pitta and allow to cool before lightly spreading with butter and

marmalade for a nice breakfast.

- Omelette with cooked potatoes, bacon and peas or with tomato and some melted cheese topping (good protein and carbohydrate).
- Brown rice (or couscous) with chicken curry; stir-fried vegetables; meat; beans or peas; egg-fried rice with raisins and a few spoons of natural bio-yoghurt. Use your imagination for other combinations.
- Chicken and avocado salad, with onion, tomato, iceberg lettuce, cashew nuts, olive oil and a squirt of hot chilli sauce.

Suggested snacks

- A hard-boiled egg. Bring anywhere and shell when desired.
- Pieces of fruit such as an apple, banana or bunch of grapes.
- Two oatmeal biscuits spread with peanut butter and jam or topped with banana or cottage cheese and cucumber.
- Natural bio-yoghurt with chopped apple, banana, orange, nuts, raisins, spoon of linseeds and a good squirt of honey.
- Waldorf salad made with chopped celery, apple, grapes, raisins, walnuts, dressed with olive oil, cayenne pepper and lime juice.
- Bowl of creamed rice/soup/cereal/steamed veg/chopped fruit.
- Plain ham/cheese/salad wholemeal sandwich.

KEEPING A TRAINING DIARY

Keeping a diary of how your training goes from day one will provide a huge motivational tool as you progress along your running path. Making a note of how far you ran, your route, whether it was hilly or flat, how long it took and how you felt throughout are all excellent details for reading back on and monitoring progress. You won't believe how far you can come in a few weeks after taking up running and the information will help reinforce your practice and keep you focused.

Make a note at the start of your weight and key body measurements. Get a tape and measure your chest, waist, hips, thighs and arm size. It's worth doing this because if you stick with your running programme, all these measurements will change considerably as fat melts away from these key storage areas!

All runners should keep notes of their training, even if it is only to write down the distance and time and their form on the day. This information can be very helpful in identifying patterns that affect your performance. Over time, you will be able to add up the miles you cover from week to week and clocking up these totals can prove hugely satisfying, especially when you are training for a specific event. They help you feel you are getting somewhere.

REWARDS

There's no point introducing a new challenge in your life if you can't enjoy a few perks along the way. One of the best things you can do for yourself as you progress along a running programme is to treat yourself from time to time with rewards that make you happy. Obviously, this doesn't mean you should pig out on chocolate and junk food at the end of every week but instead, you should tailor your prize to suit the healthy lifestyle you are adapting to. Invest in some healthy but delicious new foods and cereals such as spelt breads, granola cereals, flapjack bars and nutty, fruity treats. These are all high in calories but they are nutritious and much more beneficial than processed food. After a run it is important to re-fuel immediately with carbohydrates in order to build up the lost glycogen stores in the muscles.

Also consider treats other than food. Why not book a pampering session with a massage or beauty therapist or a trip to your favourite shopping mall to mark the end of another successful week. When you finish the six-week running programme and cover 5km, make sure to give yourself a special reward. You're sure to be that bit lighter and more toned by then so a new outfit could be the trick. Suit yourself.

RUNNING GEAR

Unlike many other mainstream sports, it is possible to kit yourself out for running without spending lots of cash on specialist gear. This is because all you really need for running is comfortable clothing and a good pair of support trainers.

At the same time, a wonderful selection of specialist running gear is now available. Lightweight, breathable tops and latex running tights help to make running a much more enjoyable experience. Once you get into the habit of exerting yourself and working up a good sweat on your run, you will find that cotton tops are simply not suitable any more as they absorb sweat and then become cold and heavy with moisture. Materials that 'wick' away the sweat from your body and keep you cool as you run will meet your requirements at this stage. Certain technological elements are incorporated into the design of running gear now, promising to help you run faster, better and longer over various terrain. Good running shoes support the movement of the foot and shield it from injury during high-impact motion.

For the more experienced runner who intends to keep running for the long-term, specialist gear is a key investment. It's fun wearing new gear for the first time and testing it out with a good run too. In fact, with running gear, as with running itself, you can find yourself wanting more and more and have to watch out that you don't get addicted!

Most of us are aware of the big brand names in sports wear and the reason these companies are successful is because the quality of their goods is so high. You won't go wrong if you invest in Nike, Adidas and Puma running wear. One brand I've particularly come to like from personal experience is Helly Hansen, which offers a lovely line of colourful tops, jackets and active bodywear.

Names to look out for in running shoes are Asics – which have a huge following – as well as Nike, New Balance, Reebok, Adidas. At the end of the day it is down to you to find what suits you best.

Running Shops
Specialist running shops are listed in the *Golden Pages* or can be found in running resources on the internet. Most of the running publications (such as *Irish Runner*) carry regular advertisements from the key suppliers in the market.

Of course the best place to start looking for sports gear is at your local sports shop. You may want a regular tracksuit and shoes to begin with but most sports shops have special sections with running gear, and staff can help you decide what to buy. Over time, as you develop a running style, you will become better informed about the kinds of gear that suit your performance. At this point it will be worth familiarising yourself with specialist running stores in your area or searching online. It is very convenient now to buy goods over the internet, with delivery dates within days of ordering.

Elverys is an excellent place to look for a starter kit, as are the many bigger outlets such as Lifestyle Sports. Arnotts in Dublin carries an excellent range of sportsgear, and I've purchased some of my staple running wardrobe pieces there. Heatons does a good line in affordable sports gear, as do the department stores of Dunnes, Penneys and Marks & Spencers. Even supermarkets have got in on the act, as I discovered recently when both Aldi and Lidl ran a special-offer week on running gear. I got some lovely running tights at a fraction of the usual cost and can't fault them for design or comfort.

Sports Bras

Sports bras are a very important item of a woman's running wardrobe because supporting the ligaments in the breast as you move is crucial at all times. Regardless of whether you are small or top-heavy, there is a design to suit you. Investing in a good sports bra is worthwhile as being able to move without too much 'wobbling' will enhance your running experience and prevent sagging. Some sports bras are strong enough to give a flat effect; others are designed to retain your natural form. There are some excellent halter-neck bras with straps right around the back which provide a lovely feeling of support. Check out the various models and find the one that suits you best.

Sports bras are available at most department stores as well as specialist sports shops, although it can be difficult to find one you really like. Be sure to try on the bra before purchase and get as good a fit as possible for maximum comfort.

There is also a fabulous selection of sports bras available on the internet. (My best buy so far was from boobydoo.co.uk.)

Running Equipment

Runners can now purchase everything from high-tech stop-watches to heart monitors and calorie counters that attach to arms, legs and various other body parts as you run. How seriously you take the many mathematical calculations that can be applied in running will depend on how far you want to take the sport. If you're interested in monitoring your speed you will love all the fabulous timing equipment on the market. Likewise if fat reduction is your target, there is a variety of equipment that can tell you how this aspect of your exercise plan is going. Again, specialist stores and on-line running shops will cater to your needs here. Talk to other runners or gym staff and check out what equipment they recommend. Some people love gadgets and feel sophisticated and cool being 'plugged in' to their various monitors. Others like to run listening to music while many like to get out in the fresh air and take in everything that is happening around them. It's a matter of personal taste.

READING MATERIAL

Sometimes it can be difficult to find material on your hobby of choice but fortunately, with running enjoying a new popularity surge at the moment, there is no shortage of up-to-date material on the subject. There is a number of excellent books and monthly magazines (listed in the Suggested Reading section at the end of this book) and some of the most informative writing can be found on internet chat forums. Everything from 100-metre sprinting to fun-runs and marathons, pre- and post-event, are discussed and analysed in web chat rooms every day. Log on to any running website and your search is sure to turn up material of interest to you and help keep you motivated on your running journey.

Log on to amazon.com/amazon.co.uk or similar site to check out the wide selection of sports and specialist running books available. You're sure to find material that appeals to you.

12

THE BENEFITS OF RUNNING

Everything I've learned about running confirms it is one of the best activities for health and wellbeing. Running strengthens the engine of the body, the heart, which is in itself a muscle that needs constant exercising for optimum performance. It also promotes better sleep and weight loss, reduces PMS and symptoms of the menopause. Your complexion will improve, as will your body and muscle tone.

Running is good for the bones
The weight-bearing demands of running impact positively on your skeleton. By stressing the bone, running makes it strong. For women this is especially beneficial as the menopause depletes bone thickness.

Running is anti-ageing
Many people count each passing year as one more reason to slow down and take it easy but a regular running regime will give you more energy to get up and go, no matter what your age.

Running is good for the spirits
Running lifts your mood by producing natural endorphin 'highs' and therefore boosts mental health. Stress levels fall as adrenaline

output drops. Many people find running a perfect outlet for hurt/ anger after traumas in their lives, such as when a relationship ends.

Running improves performance in other sports
Regular runs during the week will help your sporting performance at weekends, as running forms part and parcel of so many sports.

Running provides a lung and heart workout
Running is one of the best cardiovascular exercises and can help the body burn up more than 600 calories an hour.

Running grows muscle
Regular running grows muscle and the bigger your muscles, the more food you need to maintain their size and strength. So you can look forward to enjoying your food!

Running is life-enhancing
Running increases your quality of life by giving you time and space in your head to think things through and work out problems.

Running prepares you for the day
Running makes you fit and gives you energy for living. Waking up every morning becomes a joy as you are filled with positive plans about your fitness routine and anticipation about what each day might bring. You feel powerful.

Anyone can run
Probably one of the best things about running is that anybody can do it because it costs almost nothing. Because it is open to everyone, it can also be enjoyed as a social activity, with friends and family going for runs together.

Suggested Reading

The reading material I enjoyed in the course of writing this book included:

Delaney, Ronnie. *Staying the Distance*. Dublin: O'Brien Press, 2006.

Fiennes, Ranulph. *Fit for Life*. London, Little, Brown, 1998.

Mulcahy, Risteárd. *Improving with Age*. Dublin: Liberties Press, 2004.

Murphy, Sam. *Run for Life: the Real Woman's Guide to Running*. London: Kyle Cathie, 2003.

Radcliffe, Paula. *My Story So Far*. London: Simon and Schuster, 2004.

and the magazines:

Ultra-Fit

Irish Runner (also has a website: www.irishrunner.ie)

Running Fitness

REMEMBER: DON'T JUST READ ABOUT RUNNING,
GET OUT THERE AND DO IT!

HAPPY RUNNING!